WAKING UP WITH NORA

By Tanya Detrik

Carol
Thank you
Tanya

WAKING UP WITH NORA

By Tanya Detrik

Published by: All Write Resources
PO Box 91
Shelton, CT 06484

To Wade

There are no words.

Acknowledgements

Special love and thanks to my daughter, Tracey Hydeck Blackman, for trusting me to write my version of this journey.

Very special recognition for all the parents and grandparents of "special" children who have gone before us and made our experience just a little easier.

If I have learned nothing else from Nora and writing this book, it is that everyone needs help at times and it's okay to ask for it. With that, I gratefully and humbly acknowledge the wonderful people who've helped me in this daunting endeavor.

I am profoundly grateful to my coach, Kim Kasparian, aka Success Genie, for showing me that a life built around my dreams is possible, and for teaching me the tools to pursue it. And, to my fellow "Success Soldiers" who took the journey of learning with me, supported me and held me accountable when I wavered.

Thanks to Marie Cox for lending her time and friendship when I needed her eagle eye and personal reflections. Last and absolutely not least, a heartfelt thanks to Kim Barron, of New Leaf Design, for gifting me her talent in designing the book cover.

I hear and I forget
I see and I remember
I write and I understand

Chinese Proverb

WAKING

The room was dark, with the exception of the glowing infrared eyeball on the ceiling and the slivers of light that escaped from the perimeter of the bathroom door, which I had carefully positioned before climbing into bed, so as to allow just enough light to penetrate the room. I did that so that when I needed to, I could safely navigate the cramped configuration of the hospital room without injury. It was one of too many rooms and too many nights like this one, and there were still an unknown number of them to come.

I hadn't thought I had fallen asleep, but I must have, because I couldn't identify the echo of sound that still hung in my ears. Was it a reverberation of a noise in the room? In the hallway? Was it even a sound, or could it just have been the amplification of my startled heartbeat in my ears? My brain fog made it difficult to determine, but despite that, I knew not to move a muscle until I was more coherent, because I feared I might hurt her if she were with me in the narrow, lumpy bed.

Was it one of those times? No.

By the time I was three years old, I had earned a reputation for being slow to awaken and was known to be quite cranky in the process. "Don't talk to Tanya until she comes downstairs and has her orange juice," my mother would warn my siblings. It was true. Even worse than that, I had later come to hate being awakened suddenly. It always disoriented me, and made me emotionally shaky and sick to my stomach. It surprised me that, until recently, I had never connected my aversion to sudden awakenings to the trauma of my childhood. On that morning, I had also awakened in the early darkness. The question I struggled to answer then was- *Is it a school day or not?*

As my young thoughts began to unpuzzle, I felt some early warning system in me, a tightness in my stomach and chest, putting me on alert. The feelings grew stronger and the source soon revealed itself to be in the events of the prior day.

It was a September afternoon and I had just walked in our front door to find my mother uncharacteristically sitting on the living room sofa. Then I noticed the suitcase at her feet. It was only my third week of fifth grade at a new school. Until that moment, my relief in coming back to the sanctuary of home had been especially sweet.

"I'm already late," she said. "I have to go back to the hospital for another surgery, but I couldn't leave without seeing you first. I told the doctor he would have to wait for me."

I was confused. It seemed my mother had only been home from the hospital for such a short time. Things were just getting back to normal, or even better than normal because it seemed she was feeling so much better.

For many years prior, our family had watched helplessly as my mother suffered through episodes of pain that incapacitated her. Though sporadic, the events escalated in severity. For a long time, the pain was a mystery to our family doctor. When he insisted she seek another opinion, the diagnosis was gallstones. Perhaps simple enough to treat in our modern times, but in 1960 it was major surgery.

I hated seeing her in pain as much as I hated the separation during her first hospital stay. Even her recovery at home was frightening to me, though I never spoke of my fear. I just hoped she would get better quickly. To this day, I don't know how she knew what I was feeling, but one day when she was just beginning to get back on her feet, she was moving slowly and carefully around the kitchen when I came in from playing outside. Seeing her moving about so tentatively me made feel anxious and sad. I longed for her health and our home life to be back to normal. Somehow, it seemed she knew exactly what I was feeling and, in response and unbeknownst to me, she followed me across the kitchen. Catching me from behind and totally by surprise, she tickled me. I reeled and squealed with delight, and we both erupted into fits of laughter. It was her unspoken gesture of reassurance to me- *Don't worry; soon everything's going to be fine.*

That had been just a few days before, and now I was facing it all again.

"I don't want you to go," I moaned.

I could feel my resolve starting to crumble; this time I could not hold back my feelings. I wiggled my way onto the sweet safety of her lap despite knowing that I risked hurting her still-healing incision. It was selfish, but nothing else would do. For a few minutes I was whole, but it was over too quickly. She had to go.

My heart broke. I did my best to recoil my emotions but left the room instead. I didn't walk with her to the door, or follow her outside while she got into the car as I otherwise would have. I did not even stand at the window to wave goodbye. Instead, I carefully positioned myself at an angle behind the window curtain, which allowed me to see and not be seen as I watched my father back the car down the driveway and drive both of them away.

The next morning, replaying the scene in my mind, as I lay there in the early darkness, the fear returned. I grasped for a diversion, which surfaced as the need to answer my waking question- *Yes. Yes, when the sun rose, it would be a school day for me.* To that I was bound and I wondered if my older sister, with whom I shared a bedroom, had remembered to set our alarm clock. Under the circumstances, I knew we would have to get ourselves up, out of bed, and ready for school. My concern over the alarm pushed all others aside for that moment. I needed to check it for myself.

Across the dark room on the bureau next to my sister's bed, I could see the green glow of the clock's dial. Using that as my guide, I crossed the room, reached around to the back side of the clock to check the position of the alarm stem. It was not in the *On* position. Sure enough, she'd forgotten. As I steadied the clock with my left hand and prepared to change the stem's position with my right, my sister's voice startled me.

"What are you doing?" she asked.

"I'm setting the clock."

"Don't do that," she said.

"Why not?"

"We're not going to school," she said.

My sister's answer lacked the relief I would have expected from her, given that we would have a school day off.

"Waddaya mean we're not going to school? Why not?"

Silence answered.

"Waddaya mean? Why not?" I was agitated by having to repeat the question.

My sister's voice stumbled over her response: "Mommy's gone."

"What?"

"Mommy's GONE," she repeated.

I couldn't make sense of her words.

A strange buzzing sound began running through my head. It started annoyingly like the buzzing of an insect and then grew into the sound of electronic static, like the buzzing sound my father's Hi-Fi system erupted with when he accidentally connected the wrong wires together. It was as if I had wires connecting my ears to my brain and they were shorting out. It kept getting louder and louder and at the same time I was growing colder and colder. My legs were going numb and getting heavy.

My sister's bed was only a step away from where I stood, but I wasn't sure if I could make it there. I did. She lifted the blankets and they fell over me, but there was no warmth. I was shivering. I clung to her and she hugged me. My shivers became trembles and quickly grew into convulsive and relentless full-body jerks. On and on, they persisted. I couldn't stop shaking as wave after cold wave crashed over me.

Finally, somewhere between two jolts of exhausting body jerks, sleep offered, for the first of many times to come, a few hours of temporary amnesia, which from then on would always be followed by the same waking realization: life would never be the same.

Fifty years later, the fear was resurrected every time I woke in one of these dark hospital rooms, eyeglasses cupped in my hand underneath the blanket. It always surprised me that I could sleep without breaking them. I held them because I would never risk the delay it might cause to grope for them on a nearby nightstand, or worse, be left to depend on eyes too nearsighted to serve me at any distance.

Discerning the sound that had awakened me was no longer important. I ignored the pull of my aching, fatigued muscles, the pervasive headache that was always present in the hospital, and the nausea of my sudden awakening as I strained my concentration to peer into the darkness at the white metal crib just a few feet away. In one swift motion, my eyeglasses were on and my feet were on the floor. I was wobbly yet ready to spring. From my seated position, I could just barely make out the shape of Nora's tiny body in the white metal crib.

LIFT OFF

"I'm pregnant!" she announced.

My daughter's words split the din of the airport activity around me. She and I were on our way to Nashville, an outing to celebrate my sister's 60th birthday with her.

When I first heard her words, they affected me as if she suddenly could speak some strange foreign language. It was likely that hearing such life-altering news delivered at that time and in that setting threw me. It was not the storybook scene I might have imagined.

"I just didn't want you to wonder why I wasn't drinking this weekend," my daughter added.

Once I regained the ability to connect with the words and their meanings, my mind's eye flipped into a mental video of the Jack-in-the-box type of reaction I thought I should be having over her news. After all, this was my only daughter and her first child. I couldn't connect with the feelings of joy and it bothered me. *Perhaps it's the setting.* I have no idea how I appeared to her, or if she noticed or not.

A package of anxiety surfaced from where I had stashed it some months before, when I considered, wondered, and then worried about what it would be like for her to have a child. The package had a dual label; one side was labeled "fear," the other side "change." The change, selfishly, was about how our relationship might be affected. The fear was oddly unidentified.

When I finally found my voice, I don't remember exactly what I said. Had I been successful in turning my words into gems under the pressure to respond? I remember hoping it was what she wanted and needed to hear.

Her pregnancy wasn't really a surprise, though the timing of the announcement was. I knew she and Glenn, now married two years, were thinking of it. She'd mentioned it, and I thought her, if-it-happens-it's-meant-to-be, attitude was rather uncharacteristic of my otherwise plan-driven daughter. That nagged at me somewhat.

This was her first marriage, his second. She had simultaneously become a wife and stepmother. Glenn had two daughters, one a teenager and one pre-teen, but it became much more complicated with the sudden and tragic death of the girls' mother. Within months of her wedding, Tracey had become a fulltime step mom.

Adding to their family's trials, the past few years had also marked the death of Glenn's oldest brother, after a long and difficult battle with a brain tumor. It seemed that in the span of a few years, they had endured so much. I was still feeling raw for them. My daughter, who attacks life with focused intention in a way that no one I have ever known does, was moving forward. Of course she should, but I was apprehensive for her. I supposed that if she knew what I thought, it probably would have made her angry.

Thinking back on my own life, I realized that until she had experienced worrying about her own child, she really couldn't understand, as I hadn't. It had taken me many years to understand the anxiety behind my mother-in-law's words to me when we discussed my own first pregnancy. I was pregnant right out of high school and, at seventeen, about to be married to her son. "Aren't you afraid?" she asked. I certainly should have been, but I wasn't. How could I know?—I was oblivious.

Now, anytime I meet and talk to an eighteen-year-old girl, I realize why everyone was frightened for me at that time. Years later, my mother-in-law confided in me that she regretted what she said. Despite her own fears, she wanted only to support me. Now I wanted to do the same for Tracey. And, as life would have it, this type of out-of-context surprise announcement was not the first of this kind for me.

Nearly two years earlier, on a weekday afternoon, I received the call from my son, Michael. I was in the dressing room of a clothing store when it came. From the moment I heard his voice, I knew something was up.

"Are you sitting down?" he asked.

"No, but I can," I said, tugging at the arm of the handmade wool sweater I was trying on.

"Maggie's pregnant," he said.

He and Maggie were two mature, successful adults navigating the twists and turns of an on-again, off-again relationship. Thankfully they were not teenagers, as his father and I had been.

Behind his words I could detect the shifting shards of the emotional kaleidoscope of his feelings, as I knew he was forming and reforming pictures of his future before his mind's eye; and at that moment, it didn't look like what he'd planned. Listening intently to his voice, I knew he was grappling with his feelings and I remembered my own at the time when he was the new life wanting to be born into mine. I knew from where I stood how wonderful this news was and, despite his apparent temporary shock, how he would soon be able to realize that. What I wanted most was to create for him a good memory of the moment. Though I was as dazed as he sounded, I performed my rendition of joy, until the authentic emotion caught up with me.

It did, and it multiplied many times over nine months later when the incredible Patrick was born.

When I held him at a mere four hours old, a new magic entered my life. Many grandparents talk of this new way of falling in love. I was smitten and overcome with the realization that every new life makes life new. It was from this perspective that I finally believed that each of us is born with the potential to change the world.

Having heard Tracey's news, I was experiencing the same realization from a different perspective. Things were going to change and, while I should have been delighted, I was unidentifiably apprehensive. My reaction was not about the expansive view of new life having the potential to change the world; rather, this was a feeling very personal to me. I could not substantiate it, but I absolutely knew that what was coming would be a major change for me, and it frightened me. I was looking down another black hole. These black holes appeared in my life at times when I faced emotional situations in which I did not know what would be expected of me. I knew they came from my role of being a mother without having had a mother for most of my life. A new role was emerging with no role model, again.

After my mother's death, my father was left to cope with four children, ages sixteen, thirteen, ten, and two-and-a-half. A good part of his parenting technique, if you could call it that, was placing a lot of restrictions on us, which also included a lot of responsibility. My years between ten and seventeen weren't particularly joyous. Getting pregnant and married at a young age got me out of his house, into one kind of freedom but also, of course, into greater responsibility. I guess it's not surprising that being married with two children before I was twenty-one years old meant never having the time to find out who I was. Having too much responsibility without first discovering my own identity and personal power was a painful combination. I never came first on my list, or anyone else's for that matter. I had developed an aptitude for knowing how to make do with what I was given, how to endure things I didn't like, and how to take a back seat. I feared confrontation and could only face it if I were angry and couldn't contain my frustration. As I aged, my stunted development set me stumbling into many black holes of uncertainty along the way.

My early and most life-defining belief was that I had no control over my life. The result was that I learned not to trust myself. I drowned out my own inner voices and disbelieved them if they broke through, which turned them into my tormentors instead of faithful guides. Emotional confusion always ensued ... the black holes.

Now, sitting in the airport, my journey was set in motion. I didn't know it then, but in the same way the pressure on your ears during take-off temporarily deafens you and also magnifies the rhythm of your own heartbeat, I was hearing the first whispers of a voice that had been buried for forty-eight years.

TINGLES

The year 2008 arrived, sparking the same retrospection as always, and the disappointment of feeling my accomplishments never measured up to what I thought they should be. At the same time, I really had never defined what I wanted them to be. So much worse than that, I didn't realize the folly of it. The years and my age just kept ratcheting up. I'd be turning fifty-eight. On a positive note, I perpetually held on to the hope that I still had some time and opportunity ahead of me, even if I didn't know what I should be doing with it.

I wondered again if this year would finally be my year. What would it hold? It would be different. I could not explain it, but I felt it with certainty.

Having gotten Tracey's pregnancy news in November, I was just getting used to the idea as we celebrated the holiday season. Throughout, I gave thought to how, when Christmas rolled around, Tracey would have a child. What would that be like? I have a tendency to be aware… observant of life's transitions when I can. Thresholds in life always caused me to stop and look, as if paying attention could really prepare me for what was to come. This probably stemmed from that day I watched as my mother drove away for the last time. I learned early and knew well that the opportunity for a last look never returns. I was always on alert, identifying transitions and paying close attention, even savoring them.

I was beginning to feel tingles of anticipation about the new baby and was secretly hoping for a baby girl. This happy anticipation was shadowed by a strange anxiety, some of which was rooted in worries about Tracey's and the baby's health. Realistically, except for the fact that Tracey was in her late thirties, there was no real reason to be concerned. Many women had babies well into their forties. She was doing well, everything was normal, and she was coping better than I might have expected.

Pregnancy in my time seemed so much simpler, in that there were fewer tests and less attention given to what could go wrong. It was mostly a waiting game. It now seemed there was almost too much information. All of the precautionary measures worked in reverse on me. Rather than make me feel more confident about their health, it actually made it more difficult for me to relax. I wondered if all the fixation might also be somewhat unhealthy for expecting moms. When I commented on that, Tracey fed me enough of the current protocol to make me realize I was just suffering from information obsolescence. I simply needed to go with the flow and get over feeling irrelevant and out of touch.

When Tracey invited me to go with her to her first ultrasound appointment, I was pleased that I was at least familiar with the procedure, having more recently had a few myself. I was happy and more prepared. And I knew from having seen the printouts of other prenatal ultrasounds that what we'd see would be indiscernible to me. I was right. It was exciting to be there, but still a bit strange. I didn't feel the kind of emotional connection to the white form on the dark screen that I would have liked. I was happy and relieved, however, to be reassured that baby and mom were doing well.

Weeks passed and when it was time for the second ultrasound, I was really surprised when, again, Tracey asked me to go with her and Glenn to the appointment. I didn't expect it, because this would be the ultrasound that would tell the baby's sex. She and I had chuckled about friends asking if she wanted know baby's sex ahead of time. "Have you met me?" she'd respond, pointing out the obvious absurdity of the question directed at her, the queen of need-to-know.

As the appointment neared, I began to worry more than be excited about it, but I stuffed the worries.

In the dim light of the ultrasound room, I stood next to Tracey, peering into the monitor at the image of my floating grandchild. The knot in my stomach and its counterpart in my throat rendered me silent. At one point, I stopped breathing while the technician was forced to coax Tracey's belly and with it the baby's position to locate the full ten-count of toes. I flashed back, remembering how blissfully invincible I felt during my own first pregnancy. It had never even occurred to me to worry about the health of my babies, except for briefly during delivery, and then the only malady I could conjure was a missing finger or toe. That thought magnified the relief of the moment when there was a full count of both.

Gazing at the figure on monitor, I could not determine the baby's sex from what I was seeing, but Glenn called it. "It's a girl," he said. It would make sense that perhaps he and Tracey might have wanted a boy, already having the two girls at home, but I was thrilled. The constriction in my throat grew a little tighter and tears flowed. It felt right.

After a few more minutes, we were done. Glenn and I left the room together, leaving Tracey behind to dress.

Out in the empty waiting room, I hugged him, "I'm excited it's a girl," I said. "Though I know you probably would have liked a boy. I'm relieved that everything is all right. I've been worried." The "worried" comment slipped out like air out of a pressure cooker. In the light of day, it sounded awful and I regretted it.

"Eah," he said in the usual manner with which he passed off many of my comments, "everything will be fine."

LEOS

Spring and most of the summer passed quickly. Except for the worsening of her chronic cough, which caused her to lose sleep and even strain a back muscle, Tracey's pregnancy progressed without incident. By early summer, she and Glenn had chosen the name Nora Jane for their new baby girl.

Nora's due date, August sixth, came and went. The morning of August eleventh, Tracey's thirty-seventh birthday, arrived, and we were still waiting. Early on in her pregnancy, we had speculated about the possibility of her child sharing her birthday; now it seemed like a real possibility.

We'd all become impatient, wanting to end the waiting and meet Nora. That morning, I woke early and sat in bed, wondering as I had for weeks, what she would look like. Who would she be? And what she would mean to our lives, to my life?

I was compelled to write to Nora. I thought of how she might someday, far in the future, want to know what it was like waiting for her to arrive. I wrote because I knew it was important, though I wasn't really sure why.

Dear Nora,

My little one, we're waiting to meet you. You were due to arrive five days ago. We thought you'd be here by now! You have me wondering, who you are and who will you be. I imagine you aren't anxious to leave the comfort of the womb, and we don't really blame you. It's a really uncertain world out here.

When you await your first child, if you ever do, I will probably be gone and you may wonder or want to hear stories about what it was like when we were waiting for you. That is what prompts me to write this, though I scarcely know what I want to say.

Well, for starters, today is your mom's birthday. Will you share it? Regardless, you are another beginning and the center around which your mom and I will build another part of our relationship. It is promising, exciting, and scary. If your mom were reading this, she might say that I am making your birth all about me, but when our family expands its generations, it impacts us all.

I find it a little peculiar to see your mom pregnant, but I think she truly looks beautiful. I probably have never said that to her. I don't know why. She has surprised me because you seem to have some kind of calming effect on her that is difficult to explain. I could be wrong, but I think she worries a little that you will be healthy. These days, I suppose all expectant moms worry, because the medical profession gives us so much to worry about.

Anyway, last night, we all went to Rich Farms to have ice cream, Your dad was acting kind of silly ... out of character for him, in my experience at least. I think he is really excited, anticipating your arrival and the joy of you. You are not his first; he already knows the thrill of it all.

When I talk about you, Grandpa Wade keeps telling me that he knows nothing about babies, but he's willing to learn. Frankly, he was better with your cousin Patrick when he was a baby than I was.

Nora, I don't have lots of much wisdom to share as I feel I might be expected to, being your grandmother. Perhaps you will never know how ill-equipped I always feel, but I hope you will remember and always carry with you how much I love you and your mom. When I am able to see you both together, it will ease my anxiety and I will take pride in my part in having added joy to the world.

I have many hopes and I carry them lightly, but if the universe does truly hold options for us of which we can scarcely dream, then my dream for you is joy, whatever form it may take.

I love you,

Grandma

Later that morning, when I checked my e-mail, there was a message from Tracey.

Sent: Monday, August 11, 2008 6:45 A.M.
From: Tracey To: Mom
Subject: Some progress

Hi Mom, Happy Monday! I'm hoping today will be a real BIRTHday around here! All day yesterday I think I had pre-labor type contractions, and today I'm hoping they get stronger and closer together! We'll see. Glenn is staying home and I have a doctor's appt at 10:30 a.m. Send some good labor energy our way, would you?

To the e-mail, Tracey had attached a profile of the sun sign for LEO, which she and now Nora would fall under. Whether one believes in astrology and sun signs or not, I do in some way, and I found that day that the characteristics described therein were exactly that of my daughter:

LEO - The Boss. Very organized. Need order in their lives and likes being in control. Likes boundaries. Tend to take over everything. Bossy. Like to help others. Social and outgoing. Extroverted. Generous, warm-hearted. Sensitive. Creative energy. Full of themselves. Loving. Doing the right thing is important to Leos. Attractive.

I shot back a message to her that captured what I knew we both were thinking: "What happens if a mother who 'likes to be in control' has a daughter who does, too?"

Just as quickly, I got her response: "Can you say 'power struggle'? I guess she'll be teaching me a thing or two about surrendering."

Later that evening, signs of labor began to increase; we all went to bed that night, not necessarily to sleep, but excited at the prospect of meeting Nora the next day.

The plan was that I could be at the hospital with them during labor, but for the actual birth, Tracey and Glenn wanted to greet Nora together, alone. Alone, that is, except for the usual cast of medical characters.

In hindsight, I ask myself why it never occurred to me to inform myself about the latest birthing methods. I guess I was still thinking that my own experience thirty-eight years before was still valid.

It was not necessary for me to ask or notify anyone in order to be at the hospital for the big event. Being a self-employed marketing communications writer, I was the "boss". My schedule was flexible and my own. Otherwise there was nothing to do but wait, and when the time came, go along for the ride.

DAUGHTERS

Tracey's call came around five a.m. on the twelfth. "We are leaving within the hour for the hospital," she said. With the slow progression of her labor, I remained in bed, taking time to peer into the horizon at a new era of life about to unfold. I was excited, but there was still a lingering apprehension that comes for me with any life change. This day, another generational line in the sand was being drawn, and when I could no longer tolerate the faint buzz of anxiety in my stomach, I let the tide of change at my back push me on.

The hospital, twenty-five minutes away, was almost a straight shot on the highway. The summer morning was warm and bright. With sunroof open and all windows down, I taxied my red Audi up the on ramp and simulated the feeling of take-off with a generous punch to the gas pedal as I merged onto the highway. The traffic was light and I reveled in the feeling of wind whipping around me, making streamers of my hair. The sun, the sky and the air and were fresh and new, my spirit now lighter and more buoyant than I could long remember. I snapped on the radio. Music seemed a must, though this time it was not my usual thought-enhancing classical station. Needing to match my mood, lively pop music meshed and pulsed along with me and the yellow dashed lines that whizzed by.

I love to drive, the combination of freedom and control ignites a sense of joy that this particular morning put my senses in overdrive. I buzzed with exhilaration that kept on expanding, and then it unfolded, revealing another perspective. I was strangely able to have the experience of driving along, and observing myself as if I were two separate beings engaged from different vantage points in one experience. I've dreamt in such a perspective, but never known it when awake. I went with it, suppressing all questioning for fear it would break the delightful spell. I allowed it to carry me along as one of those poems I love, when I become connected directly to the heart of the author's intent, so engulfed that I am swept away and carried into a world far beyond the words on the page.

What happened next I can only recount, not explain. My enlivened senses exploded with sensations that grew into a feeling of an even more expanded consciousness. I can only describe it as a heightened sense of awareness encompassing a scope beyond that of any worldly experience. Was it rapture or a form of enlightenment? I do not know, but it was thrilling. I let go and flowed along in it. In wonderment, and just as I marveled that I could still be highly conscious and present in my driving, I sensed another presence. A distinctly separate energy was with me. My awareness of this was as sure as those times when you realize someone is standing behind you but no movement or action has triggered the knowing- you just know, except this was much more expansive. It was pure, flowing or radiating from very high above me and crossing my path from upper left down to the lower right, vibrant and intense much like a ray of hot summer sun, but without the heat. It was alive with an emotional warmth, electrifying and gentle all at the same time. I wanted it to stay, and as quickly as I acknowledged that acceptance, it offered something more. I felt a channel had opened and I understood it as pure communication that was both new to me and yet so very familiar.

I became giddy, as if I had just been liberated from some long-suffered constraint. It felt like freedom and yet, at the same time, like I was also being somehow connected to something. Emanating from this new presence was wordless communication. The message...I was not alone...I would never be alone again. As I felt the truth of it, I also realized the release of a long and deep loneliness I had never acknowledged. With that, the presence offered me a vision. Shadowy images appeared, stretching in a long line, reaching so far back they faded into the horizon. They were fluid and transparent and their energy was distinctly female. The one closest to me, I knew, was my mother's mother, though she did not appear as I had known her. This was all the more surprising because I had not had a relationship with her when she was alive. I did not see my mother, but I felt her. I saw, stretching back behind my grandmother, a long line of women. I understood that all of them were part of my lineage. Female ancestors. They were joyous and I knew it was about me, for me. It was definitely connected to Nora's birth. In some way Nora was connecting me to something larger than I knew. I felt also that her birth held something special for them as well.

In a flash of my own awareness, I realized with great clarity how unique the mother/daughter/granddaughter relationship is. When we give birth to a daughter and she does the same, we are connected by the most intimate physical experience in our world, as there can be no closer connection than passing on the ability to create and give birth from our bodies to another who can do the same. Tracey had passed through my body and now Nora through hers. What connection is more profoundly shared? Shared experience is the highest form of understanding. I'd missed out on sharing that joy with my mother. My grandmother and I did not share a relationship either. Nora's birth was about to re-connect the break in that chain in our family. Perhaps, from a slightly different perspective, Tracey and I could recapture what we'd missed in the breaking of that chain. Perhaps we could know some of that love we'd missed through Nora's role in our lives. This glorious feeling of belonging remained and resonated for a few minutes; then the channel softly closed. Nora's arrival, already wonderful, became even more so. I was awestruck. How lucky we were.

Flying along the highway, tires buzzing, I was filled to the brim with joy, comfort and a lightness of spirit I had never known.

It was not a coincidence that at just that moment, the country song, "In My Daughter's Eyes", about the love, joy and legacy of mother-daughter relationships began to play.

DELIVERANCE

It was late morning when I arrived at the hospital and found the birthing room. Tracey was in good spirits, but already tired from having been awake most of the previous night. Glenn and the doula were there with her.

I thought how times had changed and considered how the role of the doula had emerged in our society. The doula primarily replaced the family member, most likely the birthmother's mother, who traditionally would have tended to the birthmother. Today, doulas make the birthmother comfortable during labor, keep eye on the progress of labor and help with pain management techniques, while doctors and nurses are there to ensure a safe delivery for mother and child. Doulas have no clinical role. If I were being critical, I might say the doula was taking my role, sans the emotional connection. I might have been jealous if I hadn't realized how ill-equipped I would be in this situation. Tracey and I could be so opposite at times, that I would likely just annoy her. I did wonder if taking this passive role might prove to be a challenge for me.

Indeed, things had changed since I'd been in a labor/delivery room. For one thing, these quarters were private. This room was uncomfortably large and sparsely furnished with only Tracey's bed and a reclining chair. There was an odd rectangular tub in the corner, which I knew could be for water births or for pain relief during labor. There were also several different pieces of medical equipment and related monitors near the bed.

We'd been told that all of the other birthing rooms were occupied. The flurry around the nurses' station just outside our door confirmed that the place was hopping with activity. The excitement and promise of new life nearly crackled in the air.

This hospital ritualized the arrival of each new life by playing chimes that rang softly throughout the halls. As each newly-delivered mother was wheeled out of the birthing center on her way to the maternity floor, the staff would pause her stretcher below the doorbell-like button that when pressed would send chimes reverberating throughout the hospital. Every so often throughout the morning, we heard the chimes. Soon it would be Tracey's turn.

Tracey's labor was progressing very slowly, and without pain medication. Though she was very uncomfortable, she remained patient and reasonably calm. By noon, she'd been in active labor for more than eight hours. Using my own experience as a benchmark, I felt strongly that it was time for things to accelerate. But time dragged on and her labor continued.

A few hours into the afternoon, it was time for pain intervention. The anesthesiologist, like an earthly god, began visits to administer relief. Vital sign monitors beeped and blipped and digital graphs fluttered tracking Tracey's and Nora's vital signs.

Occasionally, the celebratory chimes rang. Another baby born and another mother moved on in the joyful process.

Around 3:00 p.m., Glenn and I took a food break. I felt guilty because, by this time, it had been many hours since Tracey had eaten. I worried about how that would affect her strength and mood. It is impossible to know or judge anyone else's pain or their thresholds; we only have our own with which we can compare. I just knew that my ability to cope diminished greatly when I needed food. I worried about her, maybe beyond what was necessary.

In addition, I was still fending off anxiety. I wanted to get to the happy part and had not anticipated how difficult it would be for me to stand by and helplessly watch my daughter in labor. Sure, I'd been through this, but by this time—more than twelve hours of labor— both my children had been born. I certainly knew that every birth was unique, but I felt I had overestimated my ability to handle this one.

The chimes out in the hallway were ringing more frequently.

Daylight faded into evening. Efforts were taken to expedite labor. Still, progress remained very slow. I kept thinking it should be happening soon, but there were no indications that it would. I seemed to be the only one who thought this should be over. I had expected to be back home by dinnertime, toasting the arrival of Nora. Such expectations made every minute pass all the more slowly.

The nurses and medical staff came and went, checking in with the doula and keeping tabs on Tracey. The obstetrician of the evening, from Tracey's team of doctors, came in. She and the nurses proceeded with the wait-and-see protocol.

More chimes- they were beginning to irritate me.

Evening darkened into night. Nora didn't seem as anxious to meet us as we were to meet her. Her progress down the birth canal was torturous. Tracey was tired and, even with all the pain intervention, very uncomfortable. I was worried about the effect of hours of stress on both Tracey and Nora. No one else seemed to be.

Tracey's father had been keeping tabs on her progress. He arrived at the hospital at around ten p.m., thinking he would be there after Nora's birth. He left just before midnight, his plan unrealized.

The birthing room was almost totally dark, except for the glow and blips of light on the monitors. It had been a very long day and we were all tired. Because the room had no real furniture and there was only one chair, the three of us, Glenn, the doula and I, took turns in it. The doula remained in the lead, tending to Tracey. In the dark, I was attuned to her every move; secretly I began vigilantly to monitor the doula's face, as one might that of a stewardess on a bumpy flight over the ocean. I was looking for a crack in the veneer of her composure as an indicator of trouble.

We were deep into the early morning hours of August thirteenth now. I felt as if we'd been waiting for a month.

Tracey was wearing a band around her belly that was constantly measuring Nora's vital signs. We could see the measure of her heart beating on the associated monitor. At one point, the monitor's alarm sounded. I held onto my panic, stopping it in my throat before I uttered a sound. It turned out that her band had slipped. The life-sounds returned. My composure did not fully.

Time crawled. At that point, if we counted Tracey's early labor the night prior to coming to the hospital, she'd logged more than twenty-four hours. This seemed excessive to me. The length of time and intensity of stress on them both, and the amount and duration of anesthetics didn't seem wise. To boot, I think we were the only occupied room on the delivery floor. We'd certainly heard enough of the damn chimes by then, telling me that my estimation of how long things should take was logically accurate. I can be quite patient, but I was losing the ability. I kept wondering at what point patience should end. This is where my self-doubt took over. After all, the doula and nursing staff were in charge. I come from that generation that bows to authority, especially in medicine, but my intestinal vibrations were telling me this was just crazy.

All night, the anesthesiologist had been making frequent visits and working delicately to keep Tracey comfortable and everyone safe. Tracey's obstetrician was noticeably absent. Twice during the night, she was summoned. When she appeared, she was obviously sleep-deprived and showed signs of having been recently awakened. Was this the reason that we were still waiting? My confidence waned.

Just around daybreak, it was time to push. After a few intense attempts, it became clear that Nora wasn't going to make an appearance that way. Finally, the decision was made that it had gone on too long, my daughter was exhausted, and the baby would not emerge on her own. It was time for a Cesarean section.

Glenn's face went pale. I know this was something he wasn't prepared for. A quick signing of papers and they were off to the operating room. We were ushered out, passing the bell on our way ... but there was no stopping to ring the chimes.

I was sent to the maternity floor to wait. The nurses at the desk took me to the room they had readied for Tracey's post-delivery stay. I called home to update Wade, my partner and emotional foundation for the last seventeen years. He was surprised by my news. He said he thought Nora had been born in the wee hours, and that I had just chosen not to call and wake him. Then I called my son, whose reaction was similar.

I sat, numb with fear. I was exhausted and emotionally spent. And I was shaken, too, by the suddenness of the surgical decision. Everything seemed abnormal compared to what I'd expected, which all added to the worry I'd been carrying but suppressing for months. I suppose C-sections are commonplace, but not to me, not in my life. I knew that every surgical procedure was serious, even the routine ones. Having Tracey rushed away so quickly was upsetting enough. I was nervous.

I didn't sit for long; I couldn't relax. I paced. Finally, I walked back out into the hallway. From nowhere the doula appeared, literally running by me ... obviously late for something. Like us, she surely had not expected this birth to take thirty hours.

"They are done," she called over her shoulder as she ran farther down the hall, "in the process of closing."

"Wait, wait," I called at the back of her head, trying not to shout too loud, but needing to capture her attention before she disappeared. She and the tone of her announcement had been so disconnected; she was obviously already in another sphere.

"Is she alright?" I pleaded.

Turning back in a demonstration of apology, she stopped and addressed the plea in my question. "Yes, everyone is fine; the baby is perfect. They'll be down soon."

Still a bit numb, I crumbled, slumping down again into the chair. Once again, I dialed home on the lifeline I had clutched all the while in my hand. By the time Wade picked up, he heard only dead air at my end. Poor Wade, there's just no counting the number of times he has picked up the phone, prior to that day and many times since, knowing only by the caller ID that it was me on the other end. Tears, throat-constricted gulps of relief, exhaustion and joy have often overtaken me--and my voice. Accustomed to waiting, but extremely concerned, he asked, "Are you alright, is everything alright?"

I always attempt to at least grunt enough for him to know it really is me and that I am not being held hostage by some evil character. (We watch too many movies).

Finally, I choked out, "She's here and everyone is fine."

Like blood returning to an appendage after a tourniquet is removed, numbness was beginning to dissipate as the stress and fear of the hours just passed drained from my system and excitement began to fill me with the joy of being on this side of the birth.

Before I could find my new legs and get my emotional feet on the ground, Glenn appeared, exhausted yet vibrant with renewed excitement.

"Did you see her?" he asked.

"No, no—where is she?" I asked, jumping up from my seat. I was immediately bursting with energy and anticipation.

"She's in the nursery. Come on. Eight pounds and six ounces!" he said, with unbridled pride.

"Oh, my God! I can't wait to see her!" I said as I ran.

HELLO

I grabbed my camera and flew after Glenn down the hallway. A few quick turns and we arrived at the nursery's window. I expected to peer through the nursery glass, but to my surprise, I was ushered inside and able to stand right next to Nora's clear-sided hospital bassinette. She was a perfectly pinkish and purple shade of girl. Her little pink-capped head was turning from side to side. Her eyes were open and she was in full motion, all waving arms and legs, only minutes into our world.

My eyes were riveted on all twenty-one inches of her, as I focused on acquainting myself with this previously only imagined character, I also found myself irritated by the brashness of the environment and the assault of the bright lights around us. I was uncomfortable for her. Perhaps magnified by my own exhaustion, I thought how disturbing this must all be for her, just having left the tucked, dark, quietly sloshing safety of the womb to be so unfolded, splayed out, and subjected to the intensity of interrogation-like lighting and loud voices. Had she delayed her debut as long as she could, anticipating that this would ensue? Holding back instinct, I resisted scooping her up and dousing the lights. Instead, I searched her face for some sign of family resemblance, but found none.

Regaining my focus and acting on my desire to chronicle the moment, I initiated her first starring role, a video production of, "Hello, Nora." In it, her dad and the nurses banter in delight over her. What I didn't know at the time was that I was also capturing her miracle.

After having only minutes to get acquainted, we were dismissed so that the nurses could tend to her. I reluctantly left the nursery. Glenn left to rejoin Tracey in recovery.

Exhausted, but elated by a feeling of mission almost accomplished, I glided back through the maternity floor hallways. Slumped on the sofa in Tracey's yet unoccupied room, I took a few minutes alone to observe these new feelings and pay silent homage to this new chapter in all of our lives. My only unfinished business was to see my daughter. I wouldn't fully relax or celebrate until I could see that she was alright. Having had a surgical delivery, she would have more to cope with than just the new baby. I waited there in the room, not knowing how long it would be before she would arrive. My "waiting" muscle had already been fully stretched over the past twenty-six hours. I was prepared to be patient again, though I decided that it had already been too long since I had seen my new granddaughter. I found my way back to the nursery window to take another look at Nora.

There were only a few babies in that nursery, and my hungry eyes swept the small array of bassinettes, trusting that Nora's familial magnetic field would instantly attract me to her. The first pass didn't do it. Could I possibly not recognize my own grandchild? Before I could scan the room again, my eyes met those of the nurse on the other side of the glass. When she recognized me, her expression abruptly darkened, shooting bolts of terror through my body even before I could begin to imagine what it meant. In a panic almost equal to mine, she began waving her hands in a frantic attempt at nonverbal communication I could not interpret. With a speed of motion that matched my sky-rocketing fear, she appeared on my side of the glass. "No, no, no, it's all right, she's all right," she said. "We just moved her to the other nursery!"

Relief.

"We think she had a seizure, so we moved her into Neonatal Intensive Care. We need her there so she can be more closely monitored."

"What?" I said. Adding to my confusion, I did not understand why she was steering me down the hallway in an unfamiliar direction. As we rushed along, the nurse asked, "Do you know if there is any family history of seizures?"

These questions added to my confusion and made my head want to explode. *This isn't happening.* My thoughts went flying to painful places. "Yes, yes, ummm my brother ... ummm my daughter's ... uncles ... on both sides of her family," I said. At the time, I had totally forgotten one of my mother's sisters had died of epilepsy at the age of twelve.

We stopped walking. We were in an unfamiliar hallway.

"I can't talk to you anymore," the nurse said. "I can only talk to the parents. I need to tell them."

Just as I began to ask where they were, she moved toward the closed door in front of us.

"They are in here," she said. "You can't come in, you need to stay out here." She disappeared into what I realized was Tracey's recovery room. I heard her voice, but caught only a glimpse of the medical staff moving judiciously around her.

I was alone in the corridor, my legs trembling. I leaned back against the cold, hard wall; at the moment it was the only stability I could rely on. I didn't know what to do. I just leaned there, head hanging in a frozen fog of incomprehension.

Quickly, my fear turned to anger. *Why am I not allowed in there? How ridiculous to be told I could not be there at such a frightening moment in my daughter's life. After all, is Tracey not my child? Wasn't the mother/daughter relationship the reason we were all here today anyway? Clearly someone didn't understand my rights in this situation!*

For most mothers, when your child is troubled, injured, or in some danger, your only instinct is to be there, for the child's sake and yes, for yours, too. How jarring it was to find myself dissected from our lifelong relationship by some officious stranger, by some arbitrary rule. I wanted to burst through the closed door and take my rightful place. But, I also realized I did not want to make the situation any worse than it already was. Tracey had just gone through a long labor and unexpected surgery. She needed time to recover. The news about Nora would be overwhelming for her and Glenn. She didn't need me barging in to the room or causing a scene to salve my own emotion. I stayed put. I had a sinking, deeply-rooted feeling that in some way I was abandoning her at the same time that the "system" had abandoned me by relegating me to the status of unnecessary baggage.

It was clear I would not go in to Tracey, and I did not want to leave my post outside her door. I was in deep water, in uncharted territory without a compass. At that moment, Nora's malady was only real in the impact it would have upon my daughter's life. I did not have the slightest idea of what the next moment would bring. It revealed itself quickly, as the door swung open with the exit of one of the medical staff. Inside the room, I was able to get a glimpse of my daughter, propped up in bed, looking puffy, extremely exhausted and very dazed. Glenn, who looked on the verge of collapse, stood near her at the head of the bed. Swirling around them were the rise and fall of the murmured voices of the medical staff. It wasn't clear to me from Tracey's expression if she was comprehending the words she had just heard, or if, when our eyes met briefly, she even saw me standing there. If she did, I felt no connection, but wasn't surprised. She'd been through a difficult time and lots of medication, without rest or food, as she had undergone the trauma of unexpected surgery. Now this. I was numb with fear for her and for us all.

Rabbit Hole

I soon realized that, for the moment, I had to be satisfied that I had at least seen my daughter's face though I could not be happy about what I saw. It was clear that it would be some time until I would be allowed to be with her. Fighting to regain some semblance of emotional control, I found my way back to her unoccupied maternity room. Once again, I called Wade. I don't know what I said, and try as I can, I can't remember what happened after that, or how much time lapsed. I don't even know how I got there, but the next thing I remember was someone ushering me into the Neonatal Intensive Care Unit to see Nora. Feeling much like Alice in the midst of free-fall, I found this rabbit hole narrower, darker, and deeper than I could possibly have imagined.

After the buzzer sounded to unlock the door to the restricted area, I was directed to a small sink where I was instructed to scrub my hands and forearms, surgeon-style. The last grain of sand falling through the neck of the egg timer was the measure for when I could stop. When done, I was instructed to grab one of the yellow, sterile gowns and put it on over my clothes, opening in the back.

Walking through another door and deeper into the area, I was enveloped in the dimly lit, surprisingly small room. This very special nursery was nothing more than a cramped windowless space. It was divided into two areas. The narrow area to my left contained two single rows of isolettes (the hospital term for those see-through open or domed incubator cribs), which lined the walls. Each one was nestling a tiny life. A large counter island cut between them, separating the two rows. There was only a few feet of space between the counter and the foot of each isolette. Suspended above each little nest was a computer monitor. The tricolored screens were all pulsing and making beeping sounds that punctuated the darkened hush.

To my right, the space was wider but shallow. Counters ran along the far wall. On the left side, various types of forbidding-looking medical apparatus and machines in an array of shapes and sizes loomed ominously. The most primitive piece of equipment was also the most captivating--a wooden rocking chair. Sitting in it was Glenn, and in his arms was our new girl.

He might not have shared the sensation, but for me it was as if I was directly connected to his nervous system. I experienced this with amazing clarity. My grandchild, his child ... our lives were now forever entwined. In the way he held her, I could see and feel the layers of his emotions ... love, joy, pride and fear--such fear. He graciously prepared to surrender Nora to me. I felt like an intruder taking her from him, but I couldn't ignore how much I wanted to. The transfer was tricky, as we needed to take care not to disturb the wires that tethered her little body to the monitoring system that was tracking her vital signs. I only glanced at the dancing lines on the screen.

I could hardly contain myself when I was finally able to touch her. Once she was in my arms, I realized that holding her fulfilled some unfinished business in my soul. Perhaps it surfaced because, had I known it sooner, waiting would have been too excruciating to bear. It was also then that I had my first encounter with life at the intersection of joy and pain.

I floated in the joy of having her while simultaneously drowning in the pain of fear for her health. It was a rapid see-saw of emotions in which the joy intensified the pain and the pain sweetened the joy.

There might have been other people in the room, but I was alone. While Nora slept, I examined as much of her as I dared to, being ever fearful of disturbing the wires attached to her, not knowing what harm that might cause. I was intimidated. I dared not move too much or shift her as I otherwise might have, as I had done so casually with my grandson, Patrick, when I first held him at a mere four hours old.

She was a beauty. Her eight-plus pounds rounded out her face, the contours of which had already softened from the characteristic pinched and blotchy just-birthed look. Even in the dim light, I could see the luminosity of her new skin. I thought of the cosmetics industry, and how no formula skin cream or treatment could ever re-create it.

I am not sure if I was aware at that time that Nora had been given medication. With a newborn, it would be hard to tell; sleep looks like sleep. But, from time to time, she would twitch, her head bobbing forward slightly, and there was some contraction of her shoulders. Those were seizures. They were slight, so slight that no one except a medical practitioner would have detected them. And frankly, I was still in disbelief. It was a mistake; it simply couldn't be true. *Everything will be alright.*

A doctor approached us. I don't remember what he said, but whatever it was, I knew he was aware of Nora's situation, and also that I was her grandmother. He was an imposing figure, and underneath his Jewish accent was some indescribable evidence of a gentle demeanor. He stood over us, looking down at us both as we rocked in the chair.

I really did not want to take my eyes from Nora, but I did, just to say, "She's so beautiful, I can't believe she's not perfect." This turned out to be an unfortunate choice of words. I meant only that to look at her, it was difficult to imagine that Nora was not perfectly healthy. My reference to "perfection" provoked him.

"She is perfect, just as she is," he countered. Then he proceeded to launch into a rather long-winded story about a father he had encountered some twenty years earlier, who could not accept his "damaged" son. The story ended well enough. I recognized that the intention of the story was a reprimand of sorts for me. Did he have any idea how much pain I was already in? He clearly did not know how purely and unconditionally I loved this child in my arms. I hated that he didn't know and also knew there was no use in telling him. I just wanted him to leave us alone. All the while he was talking I wanted to scream, Please, leave me alone! Don't you realize I am barely holding on here? But I didn't. I was polite then; I would not be so inclined if that happened today.

Eventually, I reluctantly left Nora to the nursing staff and went back to see Tracey, who was getting settled in her room. It was then around 11:00 a.m. She was exhausted and needed sleep. The talk about Nora's seizures was brief. We knew so little at the moment and stress had left us few faculties to call upon. We could do nothing but wait and try to get some rest. For the moment there was nothing else to be done. I did what I could to help Tracey get settled. Knowing I was at my limit and that there was a full and ready nursing staff there for her, I called Wade to pick me up because, though I had my car, I knew I was in no condition to drive. I remember getting into the car with Wade and driving out of the parking lot. Next thing I knew, we were home. I walked in the door, fell on the bed, and didn't wake until dinnertime.

ANOTHER LIFE

When I woke up, I wanted to go right back to the hospital, but I thought it would be best not to. As hard as it was to stay away, I knew that I barely had my emotional legs under me. I hoped that Tracey would get some rest. The confusion concerning Nora's situation left little that could be done until more was known.

Beginning on the second day, the hospital became my second home. The days that followed felt like stumbling through a dense forest after having lost one's sense of direction. Nothing we saw or felt was even remotely familiar. Abruptly dumped in a foreign land, we had little knowledge of the terrain and absolutely no idea where we were headed. Days were dark, figuratively and literally, camped out in the dim light of the NICU, holding Nora.

Of course, Tracey was also a patient on the maternity floor, but having Nora undiagnosed and in the NICU, she was definitely out of sync with the normal rhythms of the maternity ward. While other moms received visitors who cooed over their new family additions, Tracey was navigating the physical and emotional pain of the situation, along with the challenge of having to journey back and forth to the NICU cellblock just to see Nora. Her passage into motherhood lacked the fanfare she was due.

I was distressed that Tracey's own physical and emotional state went largely unattended. Like every mother I saw in the NICU, she was swallowed up by the uncertainty of her baby's condition and overcome by the barrage of medical intelligence surrounding it. There was little attention or consideration given to her physical recovery from the distress of her own body's trauma.

The second night of her maternity stay, I was granted permission to stay with her overnight in her room. Despite the lumpy sofa and broken sleep, being nearby was the only way I could feel a little better about the situation.

In those first emotionally blinding days, the inevitable question, "why", surfaced.

"It is awful to think that maybe it was something I did or didn't do that caused this ... or that it's somehow my fault," she said as we sat in the small waiting room outside the NICU. The weight of this question was unbearable. If there was an answer, it had to be set aside for her well-being.

"Oh, you can't think like that," I urged. "Right now, you need to be good to yourself. You need all your energy to get through this. She's going to be fine—I promise you. I know it."

Those last words came out of me with such certainty and conviction that I surprised myself. They seemed to come not from me, but from an indescribable source of knowing outside me. It felt like truth. It impressed Tracey as well; she has told me since that she's often thought of that moment and how positive I was.

Looking back, it seems odd to me that at the moment I said that to Tracey, I didn't remember my transcendental experience in the car on the way to the hospital the morning she went into labor. If I had, I would have told her about it. It might have helped her. It might have helped me, too. In hindsight, perhaps it was actually the source of my reassurance to her.

Down the hall from Tracey's room, in that cramped, dimly-lit NICU, were many little patients with large needs. Space was at a premium, made even worse because the census of babies was unusually high at that time. Every isolette was occupied. With so many cribs and equipment, there was only a few feet on each side of the cribs to accommodate visitors. Our visits with Nora involved a constant rearrangement of people and chairs to accommodate the nursing staff, since they had to weave their way around us to do their work.

Each family was firmly restricted to an unchangeable list of eight visitors, and only two visitors per child were allowed at one time. Despite that restriction and because they felt it was important not to wait, Nora's christening took place right there in the NICU. Tracey and Glenn were granted special permission to have their priest and Nora's two sisters in attendance. The first photo of their family of five was taken that day in that odd setting. Their faces tell a story of love, uncertainty and faith.

Another disadvantage of the NICU's close quarters was that there was no privacy at all. There were curtains between the cribs, of use only in providing a screen for nursing moms. Otherwise, babies, their parents, doctors and their diagnoses were theater for all to share. Despite the logistical nightmare of it, never have I seen complete strangers bond and behave with such consideration.

HOME

How unnatural is it to leave the hospital without your newborn child? What does it feel like to go home to the house and to a nursery ready, yet still empty? I don't know how Tracey, or any mother, could endure this.

Everything has changed; nothing in life is the same as it was when you walked out the door only days before. Now back without the baby, the only possible benefit might be a good night's sleep, if one could sleep at all.

No matter how good the care, the thought of leaving Nora in the hospital was distressing. I would never suggest that this was worse for me than Tracey; it was just different. I worried about them both, and for me, the separation was ghosted in the experience of my own premature mother/child separation.

What was worse than the initial separation from Nora was not knowing how long it would be before she would come home. Doctors' speculations seemed to indicate that she would be there for at least two weeks. We had no idea what life would be like when she did come home.

Moving from the world inside the hospital out into the heat of the hot August sun was like emerging from a cool, dark cave. It should have been a relief, but it was not. The brightness of life in the outside world was blinding. There, everything was as we had left it, but we were not.

There were friends and family wanting to know more, waiting for more news, good news. They sought some clue as to what to do or say. Was new baby protocol still appropriate? I could understand, but I couldn't help. I really didn't even want to talk to anyone outside of close family. I was on a slippery emotional slope and just too vulnerable to people's reactions. The wrong word or tone of voice would send me sliding. I didn't know anyone who had been through anything like this. In most cases, I didn't even return phone calls.

Tracey responded to everyone's inquiries by sending out e-mail updates about Nora. Using e-mail offered the ability to communicate when she felt up to it and to deliver the same information to everyone at the same time. Best of all, she could attach pictures. It wasn't all doom and gloom! Nora was a plump cutie and, other than the seizures, she was checking out to be in good health. Tracey and Glenn were very proud parents.

I admired the positive attitude with which Tracey imbued every e-mail. She delivered the news about Nora with straightforward honesty, yet without any hint that she wanted to inspire pity. Instead, she peppered each update with dashes of humor and optimism.

Now that mom and baby were separated, trips to the hospital and our vigils at Nora's crib became the daily routine. Tracey still couldn't drive, as she was still recuperating from her surgery. Life doesn't wait. When Glenn needed to go back to work, or be home for the other two girls, I would take his spot behind the wheel and in the NICU with Tracey.

We were allowed to stay around the clock, except for mandatory breaks at 7 p.m. and 7 a.m., when staff rounds took place. With the exception of the wee hours of the morning, Nora's team all but moved in. We logged a collective minimum of sixteen hours a day there. We'd make a plan each day for coverage, doing all we could not to leave Nora unattended by family. We'd hold her as much as we were allowed, her monitoring wires in tow. Most of the time, Tracey and I were there during the day, and Glenn and his mom went in the evening. Glenn would stay on until midnight or even later, if he could stay awake.

Hospital rules were strictly enforced. Only Mom and Dad were allowed to feed Nora her bottle. Given our near round-the-clock coverage, the nursing staff got to hold and feed Nora only in the very early hours of morning. She was something of an attraction for them, being full term and eight-plus pounds, in contrast to the other babies, who were mostly preemies.

Despite all the medications in her system, Nora's seizures continued with dismaying frequency and, at times, she was heavily sedated, making her body go limp, so that holding her was like cradling a rubber chicken. Getting her awake enough to eat was difficult, too.

There was, though, something truly special about Nora, something that I saw that was beyond the myopic opinion of a proud grandmother. It was not until much later when I saw other healthy infants that I verified for myself that, when she was less medicated, Nora exhibited a kind of conscious awareness that seemed beyond typical abilities for her age. She seemed more aware of people and her surroundings. Newborns can't see very well, but at times Nora would focus on the face of whomever was holding her. This was more than just staring. It literally felt like a real attempt to communicate. She was captivating. To me, she was magnetic. I couldn't wait to get to the hospital every day to be with her.

Initially, her diagnosis was broad and speculative. Unofficially, guesses about the seriousness of her seizures included personal and professional experiences and anecdotes from the NICU nurses, as well as other well-meaning friends. Stories filtered through to us recounting similar incidents, offered in thoughtful attempts to comfort us. Many of these stories were about other babies whose seizures diminished and eventually subsided on their own soon after birth, leaving no known long-term consequences. Would we be that lucky?

Seizures are most often related to issues with the brain, but the hospital did not have a neo-natal neurologist on staff. Instead, we endured the wait for the visiting doctor who could come only on her lunch hour once a week. Tracey and Glenn were lost, groping for answers and wondering who they could trust. When the doctor did finally visit, examine Nora and read the initial brain scan, she said emphatically that Nora had suffered a major stroke, which was undoubtedly the reason for her seizures.

With that diagnosis, the pediatric doctors continued with the wait-and-see approach, keeping Nora sedated enough to stop the seizure activity. At the advice of the neurologist, this would allow Nora's brain time to heal as much as it could or would. The hospital was following a protocol as it would for any stroke patient, based on evidence that the early days after the stroke were critical to the extent of recovery. No one would venture to guess when the stroke had actually occurred. When the subject came up, it was skirted. It seemed to make the hospital staff tense, and I thought back to Tracey's long labor and the absence of her obstetrician throughout. My guess was that they feared liability, but for

Nora's parents there was simply no energy to spend on that speculation at that time. The focus was on how to move ahead.

The goal was for Nora to achieve a straight seventy-two hours without a seizure. At that point, they would consider her stable enough to go home with oral versions of the medications she was now receiving intravenously. For her family, this did not present a promising picture of the future, to say the least. Every time Nora approached the three-day, seizure-free mark, the seizures would reappear, knocking us back to starting again at minute one of the count. Another difficulty was that we had to rely on visual cues to identify her seizures, and it was impossible to watch her every minute, twenty-four-hours a day. It was difficult to determine what movements constituted a seizure, as babies can be naturally twitchy, and often exhibit what is called a "startle" reflex, which also resembled seizure activity.

The diagnosis should have provided some relief of our anxiety, a window into the future; instead it delivered more uncertainty. As the days passed, we found that our hopes and hearts were taking a real beating. I found some comfort in daydreaming about the future, when this all would be a memory. I wrote to Nora. In my writing to her, I discovered things I hadn't consciously realized.

Oh, Nora,

I continuously wonder how we who love you will survive the next moment. I hope one day, when you are grown, you and I will sit with cups of tea and talk about these days, celebrating you and how you rose so far above the fears we had. I will accept nothing less than a miracle.

I had never really believed in miracles.

LISTENING

Some eighteen years before this, I had divorced my children's father after twenty-four years of marriage. Now, I feel fortunate to be sharing the second half of my life with Wade, a most kind and extraordinary man. Among many wonderful traits, Wade is one of the few people I know who knows how to listen. Sometimes he listens tirelessly to me for hours, even for days, on the same subject. He listens to my words, my tone, can read my heart, and has learned how to listen within the scope of my particular frame of reference before offering his opinion. Then he knows just how to interject his without destroying mine. When I am not making sense, he probes and strives to understand, and tells me when he doesn't.

Being male, Wade naturally sees life from a different perspective than I, and his family experiences are very different from mine. To add to that disparity, he has no children from his first marriage. We chose not to be legally married, but in every other sense we are. When we met, my children were in their early twenties and out on their own. Nonetheless, he lives with me so he lives with those relationships.

Wade has expanded my mind, my world and my understanding of myself. He knows when I need it, how to boost my confidence and make me feel that I'm better than I really am. The years we have spent together have blended our points of view much like a pair of graduated bifocals. We look together through the same pair of lenses, though often in different directions. Neither of us is afraid to introduce changes to the focus of our never-ending quest to see life more clearly.

After almost twenty years of being together, we can still sit with coffee in the morning or a glass of wine in the evening and talk for hours. Wade is my rock and also my refuge, my soft place to fall; over the years, I have needed both many times, but never more than when Nora came into our lives.

After Nora was born, I suffered many sleepless nights and hours of crying, and we engaged in long discussions of my fears. I was overwhelmed. I think it's natural that, when we are at the lowest points of emotional despair, we long to be heard and understood and even rescued at the most basic, childlike level. I think helplessness of this magnitude makes us long for the comfort of our mothers, regardless of how old we are. I did. I had never allowed myself to indulge those feelings before. Even as a child, I found that the longing for my mother was too hopelessly painful. Then Nora was born.

One morning during the first few weeks of her life, I had reached an exceptionally dire level of despair. It was the beginning of another hot August day and, being a lover of the sun and the outdoors, I sat alone on our porch overlooking the acre of grass in front of me. I am a sun worshipper, and the feeling of the strong morning sun on my body after days of living in the inner sanctum of the hospital was deeply soothing. I began to relax, and this began to release some of the pent-up anxiety and stress I was feeling. This can prove dangerous for me, as I can then lose the shell that holds me together emotionally.

I rarely get to the point I did that day, feeling so lost that even Wade couldn't rescue me. I surrendered to the deep sadness I was feeling. I wondered how any of us could face the day, the week and what might be ahead, but most of all I just felt sorry for myself because, despite all the people in my life, I'd never felt so isolated.

At that moment, I longed for a conversation with my own mother. I didn't know what it would really be like to talk, mother-to-mother, with her. I hadn't known her well enough to guess what she would say, but I longed for all the love, comfort, and reassurance I imagined she could give me. I desperately wanted to be swaddled in the caring of the one person I felt would understand me and exactly how I felt. She, above all others, would understand as no one else could. I wanted this and there was no substitute. It didn't matter that she likely would not have been alive anyway—that reality had no bearing on my longing.

I was sick of being brave. "You know what, Mom? I really need you. I really would love to talk to you," I said out loud. I'd never done that before, and it sounded strange to me even to say the words.

I sat in the sun, head bowed, surrendering to the depths of my need.

After a time, I was brought back to awareness because something intersected my peripheral vision. Raising my head, I saw it was a small yellow butterfly. We had not seen many that summer, and the ones we did see were darker Monarchs with huge wings. This butterfly was much smaller, and the purest, sunny shade of yellow. It fluttered softly, rising and falling over the garden a few feet away, but it appeared not to be particularly interested in the flowers below. It alighted, facing me for just a few seconds on a nearby stalk, and perched there slowly and softly fanning its wings. With the next effortless flutter, it air-lifted itself and landed on my foot. I was sitting with my legs crossed, my right foot elevated. There the butterfly sat facing me. It just stayed there, clearly without any intention of leaving. Occasionally, it very softly and lightly fanned its wings. Its energy was soothing, and its effect on me was hypnotic.

Minutes passed, and except for the flutter of its gossamer wings, neither of us moved. I was mesmerized. Was this another connection like the experience on my drive to the hospital the day Nora was born? This time, perhaps a message was being delivered in a tangible form. Was this a response to my plea? Was it actually some form of my mother's energy or spirit manifesting itself in this world? I believed so, because I felt calmed, soothed and reassured. I was certain I'd been heard and a response had been granted.

I felt a true sense of purpose directed toward me in the actions of this little creature. It stayed, and in the time I spent focusing on its gentle movements and simple beauty, my mood was transformed. Its presence was soothing; regardless of how crazy I thought it seemed, I felt much less alone. Spending time in nature had always been my reminder that I am a miniscule part of a larger sphere. I felt this experience was no coincidence. The butterfly, a quintessential symbol of transformation, was both a messenger and the message. It came, it stayed, and when it left, it took with it my longing.

It was also not until much later, when I thought back to this moment from a point of new awareness that I realized when you ask from your heart you receive, though the response or answer may not come in the form you expect.

NAVIGATION

Steeped in emotions and confusion, we were joyous over Nora and frightened by helplessly witnessing her seizures. Most of all we were getting so frustrated at having no clear direction for achieving her wellbeing; no path to follow. Nora was almost two weeks old, she didn't appear to be making any progress, nor were the doctors offering options. It was scary and discouraging, and we felt lost.

The process of attempting to eliminate Nora's seizures with medications was tenuous. Keeping the combinations and dosages at levels high enough to stop the seizures, but low enough to allow her to be conscious was challenging. Some took effect rather quickly, while others took much longer. Finding the right balance involved observing her and frequently drawing blood to test their levels in her system. The time that passed between drawing the blood and getting the results made it all more difficult. I hated witnessing the blood-draws.

When Nora's medication levels were too high, it caused her to sleep too much. It could take several days to lower them. When they were lowered, she perked up and was positively bright-eyed and almost communicative. I might even think I had imagined it, were it not for the photos we have of her gazing at Tracey with a look of clear intention to connect. I have one of me with her as well, and it is one of the most cherished photos I own.

She would often even make noises beyond the grunts of a two-week-old. This was exciting and encouraging to witness. We couldn't wait to get her home, and kept hoping it would be soon. I had always been a proponent of hope, but I now realized that hope is a by-product of feeling helpless. My early life lessons had been severe. I learned to work with what I was handed and not ask for anything more. It reinforced for me that I had no choice except to endure. If what I hoped for did not happen, I gave up. I've found since that there is danger in hope. I see that it encouraged a passivity in me that kept me from exploring other options, and as a result, I likely missed opportunities. Fortunately, Nora's parents didn't rely on hope. They sought, collected and evaluated a flood of medical information rooted out from diverse sources. It was dizzying to hear about.

It was at about this time that Tracey began carrying a paper notebook in which she furiously scribbled notes to supplement her memory. It became her reference. I later learned that keeping a log of thoughts, responses, names, phone numbers, medication dosages and such is a standard in the arsenal of moms of "special" children. To this day, I marvel at Tracey's ability at that time to focus, under the influence of the exhaustion and stress.

As the days passed, the lack of answers caused our frustration to grow. Tracey and Glenn were doing their own research, seeking answers and other opinions. They shared what they were finding with the hospital staff, and reactions seemed as if they were resistant to options outside of the hospital's scope of treatment. It seemed as if the hospital staff was actually encouraging Nora's parents to doubt their own instincts. When thrown into the blender of medical protocol, while you watch your infant daughter in distress, it's difficult not to doubt yourself.

The only doctor who was adamantly certain of Nora's problem was the neonatal neurologist. It was a full two weeks before she was available to meet with us, which was also frustrating and ridiculous.

Six family members and two other doctors squeezed into the tiny meeting room to hear firsthand what she had to say. She verified her original diagnosis. She was still certain that Nora had suffered a stroke. A large portion, approximately two-thirds of the left hemisphere of her brain, was affected. The circumference of Nora's head was normal, indicating that there was no immediate concern about swelling, and there were no blood clots or any abnormal pressure on her brain. That was good.

The doctor did remark that, if an adult had undergone such a major stroke, it would have left in its wake no ability to move the right side, and the use of language would have been lost as well. The infant brain, however, having great "plasticity," meaning the brain's ability to reorganize itself by forming new neural connections, was more adept at compensating than a damaged adult brain. For example—and Nora was a good one—if one hemisphere of the brain were damaged, the intact hemisphere might take over some of its functions. The brain compensates for damage by reorganizing and forming new connections between intact neurons. Usually, though, in order to reconnect, the neurons need to be stimulated through activity, such as physical therapy. Clearly this had not been Nora's experience, which made Nora's symmetrical functionality miraculous to me. The neurologist commented, with a hint of wonderment, that both Nora's right and left sides were almost equal, with a slightly lesser reflex response on her right side. There were many other issues on which to focus and no one seemed as excited about this as I was. The more details I heard about Nora's malady, the more it pleased me that she was otherwise doing so well. Deep inside me there was something that excited me about it. I felt there was something in the pure spirit of Nora that buoyed mine, despite everything that was going on.

Over and above the details of the diagnosis itself, there was additional concern about whether these seizures could be doing residual damage. Underlying everything was our frustration and longing to get her home where she belonged. I asked the doctor if the hospital environment could contribute to her seizures, thinking of the cumulative effect on a baby of the annoying noises, and ongoing beeping and flashing of monitoring equipment. She agreed that home was the best place for anyone, but that Nora could not leave until her seizures were under control. Still, there was no real timeframe or plan. The medical staff told Tracey they were worried about Nora's vital signs, which terrified her. What if she took Nora home and she stopped breathing or her heart stopped? Were we condemned to continue waiting and going along with the same wait-and-see plan? When asked about second opinions, the doctor was adamant and somewhat egotistical in saying that any neurologist would only give us the same diagnosis. Nora's diagnosis just was what it was.

When the neurologist dismissed herself that day, she seemed to take with her any options we'd hoped for, leaving with us a new kind of anger and a crushing hopeless uncertainty

Along with their research, Tracey and Glenn had already begun pressing the hospital to help them get other medical opinions, but the tangled web of protocol made this difficult. No other neurologists would come to that hospital, and that meant that, if they wanted another opinion, Nora would have to be discharged to travel to another doctor. There was danger to her wellbeing to consider, as well as insurance issues and re-admittance problems if she were to leave the NICU. The situation was more complicated than it should have been.

Since she was a child, my daughter has rarely taken any form of the word "no" for an answer, at least not without challenging it first. Nora's case proved no exception. Even if Nora was stabilized, Tracey was not willing to take her home without a plan or definitive answers about what life and the future would look like for them all.

During the next few days, it seemed clear to us that the hospital was not equipped to deal with Nora's situation, but they were also not forthcoming about it or the alternatives outside the facility, nor were they expeditious about helping Tracey and Glenn move forward. I could only guess that their attitudes might have reflected concern over their reputation, or stem from the legalities and finances of running a healthcare facility. Perhaps they were afraid or concerned that they might incur some blame for Nora's stroke. While this crossed our minds, it wasn't of immediate importance; Nora's parents knew their only focus was getting Nora to a healthier place.

Health care is a business. The issues our country faces today become painfully clear when they are framed by your own experiences. For parents of an ailing fourteen-day-old infant, the journey is difficult enough without having to fight for care and cooperation. Having to battle to get the hospital to listen to their concerns and offer possible solutions was inexcusable, regardless of their reasons.

During this period, I refused to listen to any disparaging speculation about Nora's condition or future. I refused to allow any of it to limit my ability to embrace the possibilities. It was unlike me to be rude, but I abruptly left the room in mid-conversation if things were being said that I didn't want to hear. I needed to focus on being there for Nora and to support her parents as they handled the details. I would do almost anything else that I could, but even if I had to, I don't think I could have made the decisions Tracey and Glenn then did.

This was my first inkling that, if such choice existed, Nora had chosen her parents and family wisely.

TECHNOLOGY

It was during this time that I began to realize the increasingly significant role technology was playing in this journey. Other than my e-mail, my cell phone had become an important tool. I'd been a long-time holdout, resisting for many reasons the expense and the nuisance of possessing and carrying a cell phone. Actually, there were two primary reasons: first, I don't like talking on the phone; and second, I had lived without mobile communication for my whole life, how could it be important? As far as I was concerned, life would just go on without cell service the way it always had, wouldn't it?

That, in a nutshell, is the beauty and the madness technology brings to our lives. We either move on with it or move over. After having been stuck in a three-hour traffic jam with no way of notifying the client I was on my way to see, I finally moved on and went cellular. When I did, I admit I did find it handy to call ahead and order the pizza on my way home. I did love the efficiency. Add to this the convenience of being able to call home from the grocery store to see if, in fact, we *did* need mustard—and that was the extent of my purpose and justification for my cell phone. I had become a convert, and throughout the hospital experience, it was the convenience of my cell phone that enabled me to reach back and "touch," at most any place and time, the cell-to-cell, loving support of Wade.

Not since I kicked my cigarette addiction was I consciously concerned about leaving a necessary object behind.

Despite my initial befuddlement over the need for it, I also began to embrace the value of my cell-phone camera. When cameras became part of the communications scene, I thought, why in daily life would I need a camera on my phone? Of what would I take photos, and of what quality would the images be anyway? My digital camera was challenged to take one good photo out of ten. (Okay, my skills had something to do with that.) But seriously I thought if I did take a photo with my phone, what the heck would I do with it after I snapped it? I was beginning to realize the answer; my answer at least. Perhaps not a typical situation, but having this tool always at hand allowed me the luxury of snapping, carrying, sending and receiving photos of Nora. Not only was this an easy and convenient way of chronicling her life, but even better, it was as good for me as a sedative or mood-heightening prescription. This practice of sending and receiving photos of Nora was dubbed, by Tracey, my "photo fix".

Like my initial rejection of cell-phone-picture-taking, I also could not imagine why anyone would want to use text messaging. Though I love the look, feel and power of the written word, it still seemed incredibly silly to use a voice communication device to type words. Case in point, typing the word "Hello" on the (then) numeric keypad, took 13 key taps. Just call, I would protest, why not just call? Again, the answer was revealed. It was during these trying days that I discovered many places and times in which I found myself captive in situations requiring silence or discrete communication, most especially when I was so emotional that my voice would fail me. I could text message and still convey and receive messages that enabled me to stay connected to people at the other end of my heartstrings.

Of all the technologies, there was also the medical technology that surrounded us in the NICU. It was logical, but who could have realized that the capabilities of e-mail and the Internet would be so involved in this experience?

On the Internet, websites like WebMD and others provided massive amounts of information, as compared to the resources of my childhood. Ours was a single-volume medical book with onion-skin pages that summarized as many illnesses, ailments and their remedies as the space would allow. That was all there was, except for other such reference works in the public library.

How fortunate we are to have Internet technology today. It provided Tracey and Glenn with access to information and communication that would have been nearly impossible to achieve twenty years ago, especially in such short order. It allowed them to research epilepsy, stroke and brain damage, and to investigate which hospitals in the country were most equipped to deal with infants suffering from these conditions. This technology offered Nora's parents the path to possibility. Once Tracey connected with children's hospitals around the country, she was able to establish e-mail dialogue directly with doctors who were experts in the field.

The ability to digitally transfer Nora's test results gave the doctors enough information to review her case and to assess their ability to help her. As a result, several prominent doctors and hospitals around the country became very interested in Nora's case. Without this exposure, Nora might have been like many children of prior decades, who were relegated to knowing only about local care, and discharged with little help or hope.

Within days of the family's meeting with the neurologist, and after much soul-searching and consideration for medical expertise and the logistical complications of distance travel, Tracey and Glenn chose to transfer Nora to Boston Children's Hospital, two-and-a-half hours away.

The decision itself was difficult, and executing it even more so. It took a frustrating week to accomplish. There were insurance hassles, authorizations, transportation concerns, medical record gathering and transfers, administrative and other red tape. All of this culminated on the cusp of the three-day Labor Day holiday weekend.

ONE IF BY LAND

We'd been forced to wait through the lag of hospital administration due to the Labor Day weekend. Finally, after nineteen days of no progress, doubt, fear and feeling helpless, the plan to transfer Nora clicked into place.

Have you ever planned for something and waited so long for it to actually happen that when it finally does it confronts you with a new set of challenges, putting you in a state of unreadiness? That's how it was.

The final uncertainty in the arrangements between the two hospitals rested on deciding the mode, land or air, of Nora's transportation. The plan vacillated between transporting her by ambulance or helicopter. The decision came the Tuesday morning after Labor Day. She would be transported via helicopter. We got the decision from Boston Children's Hospital at almost the same time the helicopter was about to take off from Boston bound for Connecticut. We had a mere ninety minutes before it would arrive. We weren't prepared.

I was getting my car serviced when the news came. I went directly to the hospital. Tracey and Glenn had been with Nora for her morning feeding, but had to return home to attend to last-minute packing and making arrangements for the other two girls at home. I would wait with Nora at the hospital until Tracey and Glenn returned. In the meantime, I would do what I could to get her ready for the trip.

When I arrived at the hospital, Nora was sleeping. I hesitated to rouse her. I stood there for a few moments, disbelieving what was about to happen.

Oh, my goodness! Nora, can you believe we are here in the NICU waiting for a helicopter? This is just unimaginable.

It was never pleasant to see her lying so still, pumped full of medication. Outside of this environment, there was nothing more peaceful than the sight of a sleeping baby. In here, all I could think was that this is no way to begin life. It was difficult not to mourn what should have been.

Your mom, she's never been good at waiting and not knowing. I think it makes all of this much more difficult for her.

In this case, those traits of Tracey's were turning out to be Nora's biggest asset and I admired my daughter's ability to take action because I secretly feared that, given her circumstances, I would be immobilized.

Now, because of the circumstance, I was allowed to feed Nora, which was the double-edged sword of the moment. I woke her and started the process to change her and feed her before the flight. My heart was full of pride for her as I readied her for her first trip outside the dark walls. Despite her tender age and her challenges, something about her countenance made me wonder if she'd come here endowed with more than I knew at my age.

I was terrified by what lay ahead, persevering only by concentrating on the joy of being with her in the moment. I held the sadness at bay, knowing she was on her way to another hospital instead of going home in the arms of her mother.

A palpable excitement buzzed throughout the NICU. The swirl of preparations focused on Nora's departure made it even clearer that this was not a common event. Word arrived that the helicopter from Boston Children's Hospital had landed, and soon after there appeared a blue-suited pilot and medical attendant wheeling in a stretcher. It was like a television hospital drama.

Tracey and Glenn were on their way and missed much of the experience of seeing the cooperation of the transport team and the hospital readying Nora for flight. I'd not asked, but I suspected that no family member would be allowed to accompany Nora on the flight. I couldn't imagine how we would let her go. For sanity's sake, I made myself stop thinking about it.

I did know how loud helicopters are, having flown in one as a child. I was concerned about Nora's tender new ears. I seldom made demands, but where Nora was concerned it seemed not to be an issue for me. I simply could not let her be subjected to the overwhelming helicopter noise. Also, I realized that this would be her first exposure to sunlight. She had been cocooned in the dim NICU for weeks. Realizing that she would be transported while lying face-up on the stretcher, and that she'd be looking directly up into the bright sunlight, concerned me. I voiced both concerns, which sent people scrambling to find tiny ear protectors. The medical attendant accompanying Nora promised me she would shade her face during the transfer between the building and the helicopter.

Every minute was electrified. In the midst of all the activity, I was captivated by Nora, who was lying there so completely bundled up that only her tiny face, from her eyebrows to her chin was exposed, her tiny body magnified by the large, adult-sized stretcher on which she was strapped. She was wide awake and her expression seemed to convey amusement. It was as if she knew and was pleased to be having such a fuss made over her. The fact that she looked darned adorable helped as much as it hurt. I marveled that in a situation so dire she still inspired her own kind of joy in me. I used my camera to capture the event, thinking that someday she would want to see the pictures. It also served as good distraction for me.

Tracey and Glenn finally arrived. Their appearance set the room into TV-drama mode again, making me feel somewhat guilty about the disruption for the other babies. Papers were signed. Only a few moments remained for them to be with Nora, to get updated and adjust to the situation before having to let her go.

Then it was time. Time long-awaited instantly became dreaded time, when a plan such as this is put in motion.

Not many first-time mothers must endure relinquishing their babies under such traumatic circumstances. Watching Tracey was much more difficult than watching dear Nora, who was at least comfortable and delightfully unaware...thank goodness.

Time stood still and then rushed ahead almost in the same moment. It felt like we were caught in the frames of an old black and white movie, where the villain chases the damsel in distress, but the film on the projector sticks and then jumps ahead several frames, leaving gaps in the story. Stalling between frames, Tracey and I held onto each other like two people thrown overboard without lifejackets. Being in the midst of a flurry of activity surrounding Nora was too absurd to grasp. That this situation had any relationship to our lives was insane. Passing between us in a pure umbilical-cord like exchange were fear and excitement. Nora was finally getting out of there, and so were we. At the same time, there was such fear about the way it was all transpiring. First, worry about Nora's safety in the next few hours, and then about what lie beyond. We knew we were standing on a precipice. We knew what we knew and we feared what we didn't know, and more so what we would learn next. Underneath everything was also an unexpected, unspoken yet palatable feeling of pride for how amazing Nora was, and also how we were rising to these challenges, finding unknown strength in ourselves and each other with a tenacity we did not know we possessed.

The stretcher began to roll and we followed along, out of the NICU into the hallway and beyond. Things were happening so quickly that we became separated from Nora. Hospital rules dictated that she be transported from the building to the helicopter outside via a ground ambulance. We could not go with her. We took another route.

I didn't really know where the helicopter pad was. Outside, I was all the more stricken by the sight of the waiting craft and by how many times I had driven over the white "X" on the pavement where it sat. I'd never realized it was actually a landing pad. That made the sight of the craft sitting there seem all the more odd and out of place. It looked to me like a UFO.

The late morning sun was summer-warm and the sky was bright and clear. It was the kind of gloriously fresh and vibrant day that 9/11/2001 had been in New York, the radiance so juxtaposed to the event and darkness that surrounded it.

The pavement was hot, the breeze cool and my hands were like ice. I watched my feet, feeling the weight of every footstep that brought me closer to goodbye. Looking up, I disbelieved what I saw, my knees barely withstanding the downward pressure from the heaviness of my spirit. I saw my daughter and her husband standing in emotional quicksand, as they witness their tiny baby in the hands of strangers, totally out of reach. Helpless were we. Is there any feeling that could be worse? Yes, the separation that follows.

A boulder of fear stuck in my throat, and I felt the now-so-familiar pressure of tears behind my eyes as I watched the stretcher with its tiny cargo emerge from the ambulance. I could barely detect Nora's tiny form under the white sheet that covered her. As requested, the crew had covered her face. I was grateful, but the sight of the entire stretcher draped in white was chilling. They rolled her the short distance to the aircraft and then the stretcher and medical personnel disappeared into its bubble.

In the haste of rushing out of the hospital, I'd left my camera behind. I did have my cell phone in my hand. With it, I kept taking pictures. This action saved me, and also captured for future scrutiny pictures of what we were living through but could not really believe … this historic page in Nora's baby book.

Within a minute or two, the helicopter's blades began to whirl, slicing the air and our hearts. As the helicopter rose, we did not wave wildly and smile bravely as we would have at her in the school bus window had this been her first day of school—the day that for most officially marks the true beginning of mother/child separation. Instead, Nora was lifted away from us as we stood grounded like stones. As she rose into the blue, I could not fight the tears but I pushed hard against the crushing feeling of separation anxiety and the resurrection of my wounds; and greater than that, I fought the image of her tiny face rising into the blue far above us.

GROUNDED

Even with such short notice, Tracey was able to arrange for her brother to be waiting in Boston for Nora's arrival. He'd left Connecticut as soon we'd gotten word about the transfer. It was comforting to know a family member would be there for her.

As soon as the copter left, Tracey and Glenn headed out for Boston by car. We all agreed that I would stay at home until they got settled. None of us knew what to expect there. I felt I might be more of an emotional drain on them than a help. When they had the logistics figured out I would join them. It made my heart ache to stay behind, but I took the opportunity to recharge myself for what lay ahead.

Driving home I was heavy with worry, pleading with a higher power, in which I was still not really a firm believer, for Nora, Tracey, and Glenn to all make it to Boston safely. Some 55 minutes later, though it seemed like much longer, technology again served us well. At 3:28 p.m., news came from my son's cell phone at Boston Children's Hospital to Tracey's cell phone somewhere on the highway to Boston. Her text message to me read: *The kid has landed. All is well. Doc is checking her now. We'll be there in 50 minutes.*

The experts at Boston Children's Hospital were waiting, prepared and equipped for Nora's arrival. Having extensive experience with infants who presented seizures, they began their process, which included a neurological examination, an MRI, and an electroencephalogram (EEG). Electroencephalograms are performed by placing electrodes on the scalp and recording the electrical activity of the brain. She'd had one or two of these in her birth hospital, but in Boston they were outfitted to perform the test over longer periods of time, having rooms specifically outfitted for it.

Within hours of her arrival, Nora was visited by a host of doctors who would hopefully provide more information about what was really going on.

In what would become her habitual humorous style of communication, Tracey delivered the news of Nora's journey without the associated drama by quipping in her e-mail to family and friends that, after the flight, things were going well, and she and Glenn hoped to get Nora out of Boston before she became a Red Sox fan.

She and I kept in close communication via e-mail and texting for the next 24 hours. I also sent her the photos I had taken on the flight day.

Sent: Wednesday, September 03, 2008 2:41 PM
From: Tracey To: Mom
Subject: Nora
Hi Mom,
Thanks for the helicopter pictures. Whodda thunk it, all that for one little girl. We saw a helicopter taking off from the rooftop here in Boston last night, and we still got all choked up. I don't think we'll ever look at them the same way again.
It looks like her MRI should take place at about 5 p.m. tonight, so that's good. Not sure when it will be read, but I anticipate having initial results tomorrow morning sometime. I have a sense of relief being here, not like we're floundering.
She's been pretty sleepy. I just fed her; she did well. I left Glenn holding her. It's tricky, as she has about 85 wires attached to her head...! Crazy.
Okay, I'm heading back up, will be back in touch later. I gave her kisses for you.
Love you.

-----Reply-----
Sent: Wednesday, September 03, 2008 3:11 PM
To: Tracey From: Mom
Thanks for the update and passing along my kisses.
Whenever you get this, just know I am thinking of you and my heart is full of certainty that they will soon discover just what a miracle she is!
See you soon.

Dark Light

When you see the light at the end of the tunnel, just pray it isn't a train. We've all heard that saying before. In our case, it exemplified being in Boston and waiting for the diagnosis. Up until this point we'd endured the opinions from doctors and nurses, and the speculation of others, including:

"Oh, my twins initially had seizures, but they are fine now."

"We'll control the seizures with medication and see if she grows out of it."

"The brain has to heal; you'll just have to wait and see."

"Possibly a tumor."

But in the days leading up to this, the one thing no one seemed willing to say was, "I don't know."

After just two days in Boston, we learned more about Nora's past and future than we had in three weeks at the other hospital. Nora's seizures were not due to a stroke, but rather to a brain malformation. Nora's clinical diagnosis was Large Left Cortical Dysplasia.

Cortical Dysplasia is a malformation of the cortex of the brain, which can lead to Pediatric Epilepsy, which is defined as recurrent seizures in an infant or young child. Epilepsy is defined as having more than one seizure, regardless of the cause, and there are many.

We learned that Cortical Dysplasia is considered congenital, which means it is present at birth, occurring during development of the embryo and fetus. It can occur sporadically without any obvious cause or be part of a greater abnormality. Normally, the brain cells, the neurons, develop from the innermost part of the brain and continue developing outwards to populate the cerebral cortex. The normal cortex has a very specific and complex architecture with six primary layers of neurons. In some children, this process of development does not occur properly in some parts of the brain. As a result, the cortex in that area develops abnormally. The neurological development of the child can vary, depending on many factors and the extent of involvement of the cortex. It can occur in small, discrete parts of the cortex or can involve large areas of the brain. And so it was for Nora; it was a large portion of her left hemisphere.

Finally knowing was some relief. Though still very far from any real consideration of it, depending on the results of further testing, there was some protocol that would suggest that brain surgery might be an option.

Tunnel? Still.

Light? Yes.

Train?

SLEEP OVER

I arrived at Boston Children's Hospital on Thursday afternoon, approximately 48 hours after my heart arrived there. I was armed with pillow, a supply of sweatpants, and an unshakeable purpose. I had been as anxious to get there as I was about what I would find, despite the fact that I had been in constant contact with Tracey.

I made my way up to 9 North, the Neurological floor. Nora was still undergoing long-term EEG monitoring. It was clear that, here, in contrast to Nora's birth hospital, this hospital knew about seizures. Seeing several private rooms specially equipped for prolonged monitoring was the first indication of that.

When I arrived in her room, Nora was sleeping and Tracey and Glenn were both there as well. In the small white metal crib, Nora's little body lay wrapped in the familiar vibrant pink and purple blanket she'd received in her birth hospital. I was taken aback by the sight of her angelic little face, which was topped by what looked like a white gauze turban that made her head appear almost twice its actual size. Out of the top of the turban sprouted scores of multicolored wires that disappeared into a black zippered bag resting at the head of the bed. From the other side of the black bag, another cord extended that disappeared into a wall above the crib. I discovered later that the black bag contained a weighty, brick-sized transformer box.

Beneath Nora's turban, the tangle of wires was neatly assembled and grouped into approximately 20 contact points that were strategically glued to her scalp. It looked Frankenstein-ish, to say the least. I soon understood why someone had attempted to cheer up her room by painting a huge Dora the Explorer mural across the expanse of windows at the far side of the room.

The look on my face as I stood there prompted my daughter's comforting, "It's not that bad. She's fine with it, and it doesn't hurt; it just looks weird." I was soothed but unconvinced. I'll have to see her awake, I thought.

She then pointed out the dome on the ceiling, in which a video recording device was installed. The camera ran 24 hours a day to record Nora's every movement. Some of the time, there was actually a technician monitoring the camera/video from another room. When Nora had a seizure, we were to press a special nurse call-type button near Nora's head, which would make a mark on the video recording. Then we would have to write down the time, duration, and characteristics of the seizure on the clipboard near the bed. The combination of seizure recording, brain mapping from the wires attached to her head, video recording, and our notes would be used to evaluate any seizure activity.

When Nora did wake for the first time in my presence, she appeared unfettered by her formidable accessories. I was relieved. Tracey and Glenn then demonstrated how to handle her with her stylish new appendages, which also still included maneuvering around the other, now-familiar vital-sign monitoring wires—three attached to her chest and one on her toe. To pick her up involved a strategy similar to one you might adopt when attempting to untangle a nest of Christmas lights, being ever fearful of the consequences of making a wrong move. Add to that the trepidation of hurting the delicate object of your affection … who just happens to have a "brick" tethered to the top of her head. Once I had her in my arms, making sure that everything I'd need—the nurse call button, the monitoring button, the paper and pen were all within arm's reach, was a challenge that rivaled any MacGyver episode. Success required every iota of my concentration.

Coming in refreshed from the sidelines of the medical marathon, it was painfully clear to me how weary and exhausted Tracey and Glenn were. Several weeks of constant stress, lack of sleep, and the continuous barrage of medical information from scores of sources had taken their toll. They needed a break.

The hospital housing they were calling home in Boston was a few blocks away, but only one of them had been sleeping there at a time.

They took turns staying at the hospital with Nora. Beginning that night, I could offer them some relief. I would sleep in Nora's room at the hospital. Truth be told, I was looking forward to my time with her; even the overnight feeding schedule. When my children were babies, my peers were living at college. The only commonality was that, like the typical college student, I didn't go to bed until the wee hours, making the parental early morning wakeup call almost impossible to respond to. To this day, I carry pounds of leaden guilt remembering their pleading at my bedside: "Mommy, pleeeze come and pour the milk for our cereal."

That night, 23-day-old Nora and I had our first sleepover. Neither of us knew that it would be the first of many others like it.

NIGHT

Just after Nora's 10 p.m. feeding, Tracey and Glenn left the hospital; I hoped they would be able to sleep. Before they left, they helped me prepare everything for the next feeding at around two a.m.

I was totally alone with Nora for the first time ever, if I didn't count the technician who might be monitoring us. That was both strange and oddly comforting.

I made a feeble attempt to get organized, despite the scarcity of comforts. Surveying the room, I decided the best I could do was to set my laptop and suitcase on the floor against the wall to best avoid a tripping hazard. This recalled skills learned in my years of camping, which also made me yearn to trade in the antiseptic hospital air for the smell of nature.

Glenn likes to hike and camp; will Nora? Will she be able to?

I flashed back to a moment with Glenn on a dark evening just a week earlier. Tired and stressed by the situation and too many hours spent in the cave of the NICU, he stood wearily on the back deck of their home with me. "Will this child ever feel the sunshine on her face?" he lamented.

I looked around this strange hotel and my eyes rested on the crib. Pink-and-white infant Nora, with her big, white turban-wrapped head, filled only a fraction of it. There was so much room at the foot of the crib that all her clothing, diapers, wipes, plastic washbasin, and other supplies were stacked there for convenience. I thought about moving all of it and climbing up to sleep there at her feet. I assessed the space in the crib and wondered if I'd fit there but dismissed the idea, imagining the nurse's scorn when she would inevitably discover me there.

My bed/chair near the windows was now splayed out and draped in hospital sheets and blanket; not exactly cozy, but serviceable. I'd had enough forethought to bring my own pillow. A bit of home.

I went into the bathroom to change, leaving the bathroom door open just a crack so as not to lose sight of Nora. Crazily, I worried that someone might steal her. I did realize that wouldn't be easy with a thousand wires attaching her to the wall, but I didn't think of it that way, not even when Tracey reminded me later that, if someone wanted to steal a child, they'd likely want a healthy one. Fear of loss was always with me.

I changed quickly, knowing also that someone could walk into the room at any time. The bathroom was unaccommodating in the simplest things; removing my contact lenses was impossible, because there was no counter to rest my case or anything else I typically used. I cared only that it all took longer than my impatience was willing to spend. I called again on my camping skills. Finally ready, I flipped on my eyeglasses and went back into the room.

I checked on Nora even though she hadn't really been out of my sight. I went to the side of the crib. The gauze turban accented her tiny features and made her look angelic. Tears of gratitude fell on the sheets, because she appeared peaceful and unbothered by anything that was going on. I pushed away thoughts of what might be happening in her unconscious mind. I was learning to choose my internal battles in order to conserve my own resources, reminding myself what I could and could not control.

My thoughts were interrupted by the appearance of the night nurse. We greeted each other and at that moment, I officially relinquished my name and became known as "Nora's Grandma," as in Nora's Grandma will be staying overnight and Nora's Grandma will be giving her the medication, or whatever the events of the night might require from me.

Standing there near midnight in that place for that reason, I felt so vulnerable that even meeting a nurse challenged me. I felt that I could be either buoyed up or drowned by her reaction; that's how emotional I was. So much depended on what each person who walked in had to say. Such sheer lack of control made me hypersensitive. It wasn't always about diagnosis or information or news about Nora's condition, though it was all related. It could be a smile or some gesture, and sometimes the lack of one could alter the landscape of the moment or the entire night. I wondered if this nurse, or any of the staff, really knew the power they had.

The nurse checked Nora, listened to her heart, and tended to her details. We reviewed Nora's medication schedule. The nurses would be handling it for now. Nonetheless, sleeping in the room and handling her feedings made the schedule important for me. Was I planning to do the two a.m. feeding? Did I have enough formula? Plenty of diapers? Did I need anything else? We talked about Nora's recent journey and life to that point. The conversation felt good. The nurse lingered at the side of the crib with her hand on Nora; I was familiar with this behavior and already knew that the nurses' lingering there was as much about what they were receiving from Nora, as it was about what they were giving her. Throughout our time in the hospital, only a few of them missed her gift.

When the nurse left, I set my cell phone alarm to wake me for the next feeding, though I doubted I would need to be woken. As I lowered the lights, the dome on the ceiling, which concealed the video camera, turned to an infrared colored glow. Who would have thought that the concept of "Big Brother" could actually be reassuring? My strange surroundings, concern for Nora, the lumpy foldout chair-bed and the hospital noises indicated to me that I had all the ingredients for a sleepless night and a crippled morning.

I lay there getting reacquainted with hospital nights. It had been a very long absence, but the sounds hadn't changed much, and I was reminded that hospital rest (especially without the help of drugs) is an oxymoron. For most of us, nighttime has an emotional landscape of its own. Sometimes the Bogeyman visits. Hospital nights are the Bogeymen come true.

Though I am slow to awaken fully, I am a very light sleeper. When I am fatigued, noise attacks my nerves like a dentist's drill. Here in the hospital it was the beeping and alarm sounds that got to me. Nora's hospital stays made me keenly aware of the stress that technological sounds impose on life. If I could choose never to hear another electronic beep, my life would be much improved. I also imagine they have some unmeasured long-term effect on me; on us all. I think their interruptions are underestimated, and that in the design of each piece of equipment I think its contribution to cumulative effect of all electronic noises in our lives is being ignored.

Since the moment she had entered the first NICU, Nora was attached to monitors. I'd never held her nor seen her little body without them. The three strategically-placed stickers on her chest, embellished with cartoon-like pictures—as if they could make any difference to her or make any one of us feel better about having them stuck to her delicate new skin, were contact points. A fourth, separate wire, with an ace bandage-type embedded sensor, was wrapped around Nora's big toe. Though none of these seemed to cause her any pain, for some reason, seeing the one on her toe always made me sad.

The contact points were perpetual gatherers of her vital signs, reflected on the monitor above her bed. Variations in her vitals outside of the norm would set off a warning ... a beeping sound. If the situation were not corrected, the beeps grew progressively louder. In the birth hospital NICU, a nurse was within 20 feet and able to attend to Nora. Now we were in a private room.

My phone beeped with a text message from Tracey: *"How's my girl?"*

I updated her and climbed into bed. I shot off a goodnight text message to Wade and received one back. I lay there, finding it difficult to relax, with muscles contracted by my buzzing anxiety. I listened to muffled voices passing in the hall ... the sound of a wobbly-wheeled cart approaching, passing, leaving ... a distant bell ... humming, humming, humming ... beep, beep, beep! I was jolted awake, my heart pounding. In a split second, *where the heck am I* changed to *Oh, my God!* I rushed to the crib and leaned over the bars, almost touching Nora's face with mine to compensate for my nearsightedness in the dim light. *Note to self, sleep with eyeglasses.*

Was she in distress? The sound continued to punctuate the room like audible exclamation points. I expected the door to fly open with the entrance of someone who'd rescue her. It did not. Surely, it would end momentarily, but it didn't. Thankfully, Nora was still asleep, or was she? I put my hand on her chest to make sure she was breathing. I looked at the colored numbers on the monitor and the dancing lines, even though they made no sense to me. The beeping was getting louder, indicating that the danger was escalating, the same way the beeping of a huge construction vehicle might sound just before it is about to back up over you. Still, no one came. I hit the nurse call button. "Yes?" came the response.

"Nora's monitor is beeping," I said with urgency.

"Okay, I'll send someone," she said.

Within a few minutes, the nurse arrived. By the time she did, my nerves were frayed. Nora remained visibly unaffected. The nurse studied the readings, hit the monitor's touch screen and silenced the alarm. I needed a button like that for my adrenaline. She checked Nora, checked the readings on the screen, and then gently reached for Nora's foot and re-wrapped the wired bandage around her toe. The connection had come undone. So had I.

Throughout the many nights we spent in the hospital together, this would be a common occurrence, happening at least three times a night, sometimes as many as ten times; some nights each incident would continue for as long as five minutes or more. It always woke me, and never did I remain in bed or ignore it. I could not risk it.

Sometimes imbalances in Nora's vital signs were real. At times, they smoothed themselves out to normal and the beeping would stop on its own. At other times, a contact point would loosen. I soon learned to fix them and even reset the system, though I was not supposed to touch it. Frequently, I would have to call for help and wait. To keep from going crazy while I waited, I concentrated on ways to redesign the alarms. The mental exercise served as a distraction for my thinning sanity.

Among my worst nights were those visits when our room was right across from the nurses' station. I discovered that at the station there is a master monitor board for all in-room monitors. When the alarms went off in the patients' rooms, they also did at the nurses' station. When I realized this, I was even more frustrated; wondering why, if they already knew, I would have to call.

In addition to sleep interruptions from the monitors, several times a night the nurses' aides would come padding into the dark of our room to take Nora's temperature and blood pressure, among other things. Nora's tiny arms made it difficult to get a good blood pressure reading. It often took several attempts which would often disturb her sleep.

Most of the nurses' aides were Jamaican women, with soft lyrical accents and compassionate, gentle hands. I found their demeanor and presence soothing, and I liked it when their visits coincided with Nora's middle-of-the-night feeding time. Then I would be holding her, and I could assist them in getting their readings. They would often linger to chat, and we'd share stories about our children and grandchildren. They seemed genuinely touched by the children they were helping.

If I was asleep when they visited, even though they navigated the dark room like efficient ghosts, it would wake me. I sometimes remained in bed, but learned to know from their sounds exactly what they were doing. If I thought I heard anything uncharacteristic, I was out of bed immediately. When they left, I always got up to check on Nora, sometimes finding her wide awake, eyes staring into the darkness. I could never leave her that way. I wanted her always to know she was not alone. I would put down the side of the crib, lean close to plant a kiss on her cheek, and sing her back to sleep. This may have helped me more than it did her.

It always bothered me that my bed was lower than the crib, because I could not see her when I was lying there. Even though I slept with my eyeglasses in my hand, the lack of vantage point caused me to rise more often than I might have, just to check on her. Sometimes, though, when her little arm was splinted for an IV, I would wake up to see her waving it in the air, just barely visible above the bars.

Overnight feedings were my sacred moments with Nora. The rewards far outweighed the circumstances for me. I could argue about which of us actually received the most nourishment, though our hungers were vastly different. I don't know what other grandmothers experience. For me, holding Nora close against me satisfied some primal need.

These feedings took some concentrated preparation because I was alone in the room with Nora.

Before I could pick her up to feed her, I'd have to have everything meticulously prepared and staged. I would carefully gather and set within arm's reach the bottles, nurse call button and burp cloth, as moving around the room with her in my arms was not possible with her attachments.

The rocking chair had to be moved very close to the crib to allow enough slack in the transformer box wires and the wires on her chest and foot. If they were not carefully arranged around her before I attempted to pick her up, they could become disconnected or tug on her delicate body. I also needed to be maneuver carefully to protect the port and appendage that was splinted for her IV. She needed these in case of emergency.

I always carefully balanced a pillow over the hard wooden arm of the chair to protect her head as it rested in the crook of my elbow. Most often, the pillow would shift and fall as I settled into the chair. I could never reach it with her in my arms, so I would have to get up, lay her back down and start all over again. At four in the morning, it felt like an Olympic sport for which I'd not been trained.

Inevitably, the monitoring system warning beeps would chime in, adding its serenade to mine.

RELEASE

The day before Nora was scheduled to be released from the Boston hospital, Glenn returned to the hospital and I went home. It was difficult for me to be back at home and so distanced after having been so involved in everything. To ease the disconnection, I kept in close contact with Tracey.

During her one-week stay in Boston, Nora had attracted much attention. She had undergone countless tests, been observed and/or examined by scores of doctors, nurses, technicians and medical students, and was visited by most every attending neurologist, neurosurgeon and epileptologist. An epileptologist is a neurologist who has taken at least an additional two years of specialized training in epilepsy and treats only epilepsy. From them, Tracey had chosen Dr. Ann Bergin, a pediatric epileptologist, for Nora's primary physician in Boston. She would continue to follow Nora's progress at home and act as Tracey's contact with the rest of the team in Boston. Tracey appreciated both her expertise and compassion. We'd seen Dr. Bergin smile easily and often, and at moments saw a glistening of tears during conversations about Nora's health. She was Irish, with a brogue and a presence that was calming. Based on reports from Tracey at home, Dr. Bergin would take the lead in prescribing and adjusting Nora's cocktail of anti-seizure medications. Tracey and Glenn would keep her updated about Nora's condition and reaction to the meds. If there were significant changes in her seizures, Dr. Bergin would order blood work to be done in Connecticut, review the test results in Boston and make the necessary changes.

Nora's final test on the day of her release was the car seat test. As with any hospital, parents of newborns are required to bring the baby's car seat into the hospital, where it is inspected and adjusted for fit. I am not sure if it was because the ride home was a two-and-a-half-hour journey, but Nora's test involved having her remain in the seat for an extended period of time.

Tracey sent me a photo fix of the event. In it, bright-eyed Nora looked delighted, harnessed in her seat. She looked as if she really understood the meaning of what was happening . . . that she was going home. Her face reflected excitement and she was vocal about it. *She's quite chatty*, said Tracey's text message to me. *Talking to anyone who will pay attention.* I felt the excitement from where I was. Finally, something was as it should be.

One week after she had arrived in Boston, two days shy of one month old, Nora was on her way home for the first time. I waited anxiously. I'd left flowers and balloons in their kitchen at home. I wanted to make up for the fanfare Tracey had missed; the joy we should have celebrated a month ago. I wanted to be there when they got home, but I stayed put.

Finally came the message that lit up my phone and my heart: *Be home in ten minutes* it said. It was mid-evening and already dark outside. It was the end of another long and tiring day, but they were home.

The date was September 11th, 2008. Hard to forget.

Despite all that had happened in a month, there was much to be thankful for. The simple joy of knowing Nora and her parents were home in their own beds without monitors, beeping or doctors. It was the best rest any of us had had in weeks.

READJUSTING

Having Nora home was the beginning of another kind of life. At home, there was no medical staff at arm's reach. In a message to family and friends, Tracey quipped that Nora had begun to realize that she would not have a staff of nurses and neurologists at her beck and call day and night. In fact, I think it was Tracey who might have missed them, for good reason.

Nora's seizures were the dominant focus of the days. When they appeared, she looked as if a small electrical current had been applied to her body. They varied in intensity, and could manifest as full-body contractions, lasting from a moment to several seconds at a time, or they could look like nothing more than exaggerated twitches. They always came in clusters. The length of time that each cluster lasted and the number of seizures per cluster varied greatly. She could experience as many as 80 seizures in a 40-minute timeframe. The episodes could repeat every few hours, or she could go 10 to 12 hours without any at all. If there was such a thing, a good day meant five clusters; a bad day could be 25 or more. There was no predictable pattern, and nothing external set them off. They could happen at literally any time; in the middle of a feeding, or while she was cooing— even during sleep. At best, they could come and go leaving her totally unaffected. When intense, they upset her; agitating her enough to make her cry. Once in that state, they would interrupt her crying, which angered her and caused her to cry harder until the point of exhaustion. Many times just as she would fall asleep, the "electricity" would awaken her.

Whenever she felt it got too much for Nora, Tracey had an additional sedative she could give her. At those times, we wished we had some for ourselves.

It was still important to track each seizure, in order to monitor the effectiveness of the meds. Wherever Nora was, there was also the Notebook. Each day started a new page. We'd record, as we had in the hospital, the time each episode started and ended; in between we added a hash mark for every individual seizure. Each hash mark told another wordless story in the book of our helplessness. And the back of our minds was also the ever-nagging concern about what further damage the seizures and the medications might be causing.

I cared for Nora during many episodes. When they occurred, I held her, rocked her, walked, sang and soothed her, or tried to. There didn't seem to be any comfort in it, or any magic as I often wished for. It may have only helped me, and then only a little. I prayed, though not a believer in prayer. I wanted to believe that if I brought all my energy, focused love and concentration to it, I could make them go away.

I witnessed and recorded hundreds upon hundreds of seizures, but none more impossible to bear than the first time I saw that, with the strongest jolts, her sweet little toes would cramp into the most impossibly contracted curl. I know each of us took turns crying with her.

All in all, it was good to be home, but getting back to normal life wasn't easy. While captive in the hospital, we could focus totally on Nora and our concern for her. To call that a luxury sounds insane, but Tracey and I agreed that, in some strange way, it was. At home, the demands of daily life required time, attention and energy that we often didn't have.

The intensity of Nora's first month of life gave way to trying to establish some routines at home, which is difficult with any new baby; for Nora and family, this was only the first stretch of a marathon, which they had no idea how far it would be or if there were a finish line.

What they did have, at least, was a diagnosis, doctors, and a hospital that was familiar with Nora's case. And they had an extraordinarily beautiful, bright, and otherwise healthy daughter ... actually, three daughters. And that was yet another wrinkle in the fabric of life with Nora's illness—there were two other children in the household. Their lives would have been disrupted sufficiently by having a newborn in the house. Like all contemporary teens and pre-teens, these girls had their own schedules, agendas, and needs. And it had been only two years since they'd lost their mother. Their house was already a revolving door of activity before Nora arrived. Now Tracey and Glenn really had their hands full. In the consternation of keeping this chaotic life as balanced as possible, it seemed that someone was always taking one on the emotional "chin" in the process. And yet, somehow they stitched together a new family.

Almost immediately, the revolving door spun faster, bringing in visiting nurses and administrators from the state's Birth-to-Three services. Tracey included me in the meetings and I was there for as many of them as I could possibly attend. I am a private person; even though it wasn't my home or my baby, I still found it uncomfortable and invasive letting all those people in. We'd hardly gotten our emotional arms around the situation ourselves. For me, engaging in discussions about Nora with strangers outside the medical field was uncomfortable. In the hospital it seemed natural, but home was a sanctuary. If Tracey felt the same, she never flinched.

During these meetings, we'd all sit in the living room with Nora right there, and discuss her. Some of the visitors didn't even look at her. For some of them it was a process by the book. Certainly I was aware that she was one of many on their calendars, but it mostly felt like we were all alone.

I watched Tracey and Glenn question and be questioned. I felt and saw hope and heartbreak. They were interviewed and inundated with information, forms, facts and speculations. What I loved so much was their open and enduring expressions of unbridled pride in their daughter.

It surprised me that these agency people knew as much as they did about children like Nora. Of course, they really didn't know Nora; not the real Nora. When they left, they left behind more forms, questionnaires and calls for Tracey to make, adding more weight to the landslide.

Except for her seizures, it was impossible for anyone but a professional to detect any difference between Nora and any average infant. Yet, these people already had ideas about what she would need in terms of assistance. Still, they shared few answers as to what we could expect in terms of Nora's development.

I'd watched endless examinations of Nora in the hospital, and before they spoke, I learned from doctors' faces that she definitely exhibited differences from typical babies.

What we learned was that Nora's brain malformation caused her to be afflicted with hemiplegic cerebral palsy.

Hemiplegic or hemiplegia means that the paralysis is on one vertical half of the body- the side opposite the affected part of the brain; the right hemisphere controls the left side.

It was clear right at birth that Nora was not paralyzed on one side. Now knowing the diagnosis, that seemed to me to be a miracle. Based on the condition of one side of her brain, she should have been. Nora's exact physical diagnosis is called hemiparesis, which means a weakening on one side of the body...her right side (because her left hemisphere was affected). The list of possible effects of her hemiparesis was long and much too early to assess; stiffness and weakness in muscles on one side of the body, only using one hand during play or favoring one hand, keeping one hand in a fist, difficulty with walking and balance, difficulty with fine motor tasks like writing or using scissors, delay in reaching expected developmental milestones such as rolling over, sitting up, crawling, or smiling...we'd delightfully witnessed very early there were no issues with smiling! But her right side was weaker. She did hold her right arm closer to her body with that hand clenched, thumb inside against her palm. Her right leg and ankle were more "relaxed" than the left and less responsive.

She was also diagnosed as having generally "low muscle tone," which wasn't apparent to me. This was the "relaxed" response I optimistically thought was due to being drugged by her medications. This turned out to be my naïve, wishful thinking.

There was much to learn and pay attention to, but the good news was that hemiplegia is not a progressive condition.

Wasting no time at all, Nora began physical therapy almost immediately. The therapist would come to the house three times a week. These appointments filled up the calendar and our heads, and Tracey's notebook swelled with related notes. We were all learning that there was much more to learn.

I wanted to be at every physical therapy appointment. I'd once had therapy for a shoulder injury, but I could not imagine how it worked with an infant. Living ten minutes from Tracey's house made it convenient to be there and difficult to stay away. At home, I found myself constantly distracted and unfocused. Nora and Tracey were still the focal point and, while I attempted to exercise restraint and focus on my business, I spent more time thinking about what I should be doing than actually doing it. I felt the constant pull of my attention and the therapy appointments were a reason to give in. I'd vow to only go for the appointment, but would end up staying for hours. Back at home, I would inch my way through the day, conversing with Tracey via phone calls, e-mails and text messages.

By the time Nora was ten weeks old, she had been "introduced" to scores and scores of people, but hardly any of her extended family and friends had met her. Visitors were being held back to keep Nora safe from any other compromises to her health. Sadly, Tracey still could not enjoy the attention and adoration most new mothers and their babies enjoy. I think she was overwhelmed and exhausted, with so little emotional breathing room. I do not know how my daughter, or any mom in a similar situation, manages to push forward.

Tracey is a tenacious advocate for her daughter, and a master planner. With all the attention to Nora's needs, hers were neglected. Some of that is motherhood, but to this extent it was tragic; both her and Glenn's abilities in this unnatural state of being appeared to me incredible.

I was amazed by the many acts of kindness bestowed on them, and also angered by the thoughtlessness of others. I felt helpless witnessing their frustration over confused communications, complex health insurance issues, and the knowledge they were facing financial concerns they simply could not have foreseen, and with which I couldn't help.

Along the way, I heard people tell Tracey, "God only gives us what we can handle." Was that supposed to be comforting? I tried to extend the benefit of the doubt in that it was probably said with that intention, or as a backhanded compliment of her strength. Did these people really believe that only the strong are burdened? I tend to believe that when confronted with challenge and tragedy, some people dig deep to find the strength, while others do not.

People can say a lot of unfortunate things when they don't know what to say. I guess if I could give any reflection on what it is like to be in that kind of situation, I would suggest sending a caring message without expecting a call back, or even an email or text. Just know that the thought and time taken to communicate that you care is what will truly count. If you do connect in person: How are you doing? How can I help? What do you need? Can I bring you dinner?" are appropriate questions, followed up with purely sympathetic listening.

Living in "Noraville," as Tracey aptly dubbed it, was literally like having moved to a strange town.

As we limped through October, you might say that we were becoming somewhat accustomed to seeing Nora have seizures, which even sounds strange. It was never easy.

The entire fall of 2008 was lived in a kind of slow-motion; one step forward, two steps back, good days, bad days, and lots of sleepless nights for our circle of hearts. Tracey's everyday life was packed with phone calls to Nora's doctors and making appointments with new specialists whose specialties we had not previously heard of and still found unpronounceable. Tracey investigated state and federal assistance programs, juggled appointments with early intervention assessments and therapists, as well as fielded pediatrician calls and scheduled visits.

Most disturbing were the never-ending, ever-frustrating calls to the insurance company. When your life is overloaded with a sick baby, what could be more exasperating than fighting for insurance coverage for her? Some of my angriest moments occurred while overhearing Tracey's attempts to get coverage, payment or verify pre-qualification of coverage. One call in particular that I happened to overhear made my blood boil.

"Oh, I am sorry," Tracey said to the claims person, "I know you go through a lot, it must be difficult for you, but is there anything I can do on this end to help you get this settled?"

The bill for Nora's helicopter transport was in question for a long time; though it had been pre-approved at the time, it still became a financial issue. In another instance, a pre-approval was submitted for care and was granted. The care was provided and Tracey received the check from the insurance company. A few weeks later, the insurance company told her she had to return the money because they had made an error about the coverage. The unnecessary idiocy, undue hardship and helpless frustration seemed nothing less than a criminal bait-and-switch tactic in my estimation.

Sometime after that, I declined a copywriting assignment for a very large health insurance company. I found that my recent experience meant I just could not think of working for them.

BLEEDING

At ten weeks old, it was wonderful that, despite the seizures, Nora was otherwise healthy. She always delighted us with her responsive cooing, smiling and typical baby behavior.

Because she was growing rapidly and her medication dosages needed to be adjusted to her weight, patterns in this process began to emerge. Every few weeks, she "broke through" her medications. The seizures would grow more frequent and often more intense and the doctor would order more blood work before she would prescribe anything.

The draws had to be done either before her morning or evening medications. Evening was much easier, but that meant that her evening feeding would be delayed until after her blood was drawn. I didn't like Tracey taking Nora by herself, and most often Glenn was working late or needed to be at home for the other two girls. When he could not go with Tracey, I did.

We never had much advance warning, as Nora's condition could change markedly in a few hours. Even if she worsened in the morning, we'd have to wait until the end of the day for the blood test. By that time, Nora would usually be seizing even more. The fact that this was also our dinnertime made it all the more taxing. We'd never have time beforehand to fortify ourselves; we were always there while "running on empty."

Tracey chose to use the lab at the local hospital because it stayed open later in the evening than other labs, and because the other labs were not adept at dealing with babies; it sometimes took them as many as five attempts to hit Nora's vein, which absolutely infuriated me. The hospital lab had one skillful technician who could do it on the first try.

On one such day, we arrived at the hospital lab at around 5 p.m. We knew we'd likely be there until 7 p.m. because there was usually some annoying red tape that would hold up the process. Regardless of how proactive Tracey was in communicating with the team in Boston, there was always some issue to resolve at the desk. This time, the lab had no record of a doctor's script from Boston, causing Tracey to spend 30 minutes on her cell phone, while we all waited. By then, it was after the doctor's regular office hours, but she finally tracked down someone in Boston who could help. Even after the red tape was taken care of, we still waited. We hoped that when we did get in, they would have an infant-sized needle on hand, or we would have to wait even longer for someone to go in search of one.

We'd learned to work as a team in this. Tracey handled the details. I concentrated on Nora who, with the late hour, was getting hungrier by the minute, making us both anxious. She was cranky and the pacifier frustrated her instead of soothed her. To distract her, I talked, sang and walked the hallways, being careful not to stray too far for fear of missing our turn or the arrival of the technician who had gone in search of the coveted needle.

When we were called, I laid Nora down on the table. The white paper that covered it made a crinkling sound beneath her and she wiggled with delight, making us both smile.

In addition to Nora, there were four of us and her stroller in the tiny room and we carefully shifted multiple times to allow the technician to prepare her needles and tubes. She knew Nora from previous visits. She was a sweet, petite, compassionate Latin woman. She was the best, which meant that she was spared the precautionary scolding from me that others got. This scolding was new behavior for me and it surprised me. With my typically passive temperament I was astonished to hear myself say things like, "One stick, right? You've got to get it the first time; her veins are so small." The seriousness and imperiousness of my tone never belied the fact that, until Nora's birth, this behavior would have been viewed as utterly uncharacteristic of me.

I reluctantly moved away from the table to make way for the technician at Nora's side. The only place left to stand was at Nora's head. I looked at Tracey...which one of us would take the spot tonight? She nodded. My turn. I moved and then I leaned over her, my face upside down to hers. She raised her eyes to mine with interest. "Hi, my beauty," I said. I saw they were ready to start and as soon as they held down her arm it began. At her tender age, Nora had already learned to associate the feeling of the rubber tourniquet around her arm as a sign of what was to come. *Arrrggggghhhh, I hate this.* Her earlier squirms of delight turned to struggle, and the sadness of betrayal squeezed her face. I put a hand on each side of her head and leaned down close, talking to her all the while, and then began to sing, "The wheels on the bus go 'round and 'round." *I hope tonight will be easy and quick. If it is, she'll just cry for a bit.* It was not. It took longer. My song was rendered useless by the volume of her crying, while we were locked in a process that seemed, to me, to last forever. The technician remained focused and calm. Nora was so upset that, by the time the tubes were filled with her blood, she was "air crying" for so long I was afraid she'd stopped breathing. My tears fell on the white paper beneath her head…I didn't care what anyone thought, yet I wished I could be stronger for Nora and Tracey. The bandage went on her arm and the others moved away. By the time Tracey moved in to sooth her, Nora had gone almost instantaneously from crying to passed-out-asleep.

Will it be this way forever?

MESSENGERS

It was late October, and one of those days which comes on the tail of one of those weeks. This time, Tracey, Nora and I had been back in Boston Children's Hospital for four days. We were there after a week at home, watching Nora's seizures worsen. Her crankiness and our helplessness had only added to the fatigue we were feeling.

It had been a week of questioning. Wondering and struggling to decide whether or not to make the trip, and how long we could delay making the decision and packing just in case. When it became clear we must go, we set the plan in motion and wondered how long we'd be staying. The only certainty was uncertainty.

We'd been coping with as many as seven bad nights of sleep and too many hours in the hospital. We were sick of being trapped in the ten-by-ten-foot room and my thoughts paced like a thick-coated animal caged in the desert sun.

We were weary from waiting for the changes in medications to grant Nora some relief and I was darned cranky because the night nurse wasn't one of my favorites. I hated the arid hospital climate and little things like the static in the sheets and my hair, and the crawling dryness of my skin were all driving me crazy. I was sick of every available food choice; I was eating badly and feeling it. It sucked.

It seemed, though, that some earthly god was present, sending a masseuse to give free chair massages to the parents on our floor. I was the first to sign up, adding Tracey's name to the list as well. The hospital tries to do as many things as it can for the children and their caregivers, all trapped there. There were visits from therapy dogs, special ice-cream sundae carts, and other treats and entertainment that appeared several afternoons each week.

Out in the hallway there was live music. I believe, as they did, in its power to soothe us as nothing else can. I'd brought music into Nora's hospital room for that reason. I'd read that it can also stimulate the brain and heal on a molecular level. I believe this and I could actually imagine it making the synapses in the brain tap dance and the feel-good juices in the body flow.

Tracey had gone for her chair massage. I heard the music in the hallway and it called me like the Pied Piper of Hamlin. Nora was unhappy and fussy and I hoped it would help her settle down. With permission from the nurse, I disconnected her from the monitors and carried her wrapped little body down the hallway to join others there, who were gathered around a woman playing a harp that looked unusually large in the small space.

As I stood listening, I remembered having seen scenes like this pictured in newspapers, on television news reports and in movies ... a gaggle of pajama-clad kids, of all ages and with all manner of illness, assembled for a few moments of fun and pseudo-normalcy in the odd surroundings. I couldn't believe I was standing in one of those scenes ... that this was part of my life.

To my left was a teenager in a wheelchair. Her body was quite twisted and her head hung and then rose in movement that demonstrated lack of physical control. Cognitively, she appeared not to relate to the world around her, yet clearly she was responding in her own way to the music. I made eye contact with her mother and did my best to send affection with my eyes.

Until then, I had dismissed the harp as an unimportant and silly instrument. Now its tones resonated deeply within me and I realized why it is always depicted as the instrument of angels. I was carried away, gliding on its vibrations. I watched the musician's hands, amazed, as she coaxed the release of my deepest sadness. Is it the pleasure of the music that makes the pain much worse or the other way around? It soothed and unsettled at the same time. I could only call it a "bad kind of good" and I wondered if my contradictory feelings were the reason why the music did not calm Nora as I'd hoped it would.

Back in the room, the three of us somehow made it to the dusk of the day, which comes early in fall. Nora was finally sleeping. The chaplain, a female nun who otherwise visited in the morning, entered the room. I had seen her before, yet I was still startled by how petite she was. Standing next to Tracey's five-foot-nine-inch frame, her stature was so small that she literally looked like a child herself, but her presence belied her size. What I felt from her reminded me of my aunt Margaret, my mother's sister. She and this chaplain exuded certainty or confidence devoid of ego that emanates from some deep knowledge that they are one with their mission in life. They both had an authenticity that made one feel safe, calm, and even honored just being in their presence. The chaplain told Tracey that she was late in visiting because it had been a difficult day at the hospital. We could guess what she meant. She was not a young woman and I could feel her weariness, yet she was one hundred percent present with us.

She inquired about Nora's health and then spoke of God's presence with us. I did not share the feeling.

After a small pause, she startled me with a simple question for Tracey: "What do you want for Nora? What do you want us to ask God for?"

Tracey's answer came without hesitation. Of all the answers I might have expected, I did not anticipate this one, but when I heard it, I knew it came from the depths of my daughter's being. It reflected the pure essence of this child of mine … of who I know her to be. It was, in all her life with me, the most heartfelt and honest response I have ever heard her utter: "I just want her to be happy," she said.

RE-ENTRY

By the time November rolled in, Tracey was doing her best to go back to her full-time job on a part-time schedule. Even though she could do much of it from home that always sounded easier that it was. I helped out with Nora as often as I could and sometimes we'd tag-team, taking turns getting our respective work done.

When we weren't together, e-mail was the form of communication because it also served to document our schedules as memory often failed us.

Sent: Tuesday, November 3, 2008 12:11AM
From: Tracey To: Mom
Subject: Nora's November Schedule
Hi Mom,
Just filling you in. Nora will see the epilepsy doctor in Hartford on Wednesday, November 19th. From there, we'll drive to Boston and stay overnight, and Nora will have her MRI in Boston on Thursday. After the MRI, she'll be admitted back to the epilepsy floor for three days of long- term EEG monitoring, which means we will be staying there for three or four days. Would you like to join us?
While we are there, we'll also talk with the epilepsy neurosurgeon to discuss whether or not Nora is a good candidate for surgery.
I know, it's a scary prospect, but it may be the best alternative for her, and the best chance we have at stopping the seizures altogether. We pray that she is a candidate, but we'll learn more about that. From what we know at this point, surgery could take place sometime before her first birthday. I guess we'll know more when we talk to the doctor.

Through her investigation of it, Tracey had passed on information about the surgical procedure, but I resisted the details, letting only some of it filter in. Since I had the luxury of not having to make the decision, I didn't have to deal with even the thought of it unless I was absolutely forced to. I marked my calendar for the visit to Boston, but things didn't go exactly as planned. During the week prior to the appointment in Boston, Nora's seizure activity escalated beyond what we had witnessed to that point. It was a consistently gradual increase; there were new meds and we waited for them to take effect, but they did not make a difference. This was a first time that had been the case, and Tracey was struggling with what to do about it.

Because Nora did have the appointment already scheduled for the following week in Boston, Tracey wondered if things could wait until then, or if she should try the local hospital for some temporary relief, or should we take her to Connecticut Children's Medical Center in Hartford? Tracey had connected with them a few weeks earlier, attempting to establish coordination of care between them and Boston for the pure convenience of having a local resource. They were better staffed to deal with epilepsy than Nora's birth hospital. Or, should we just drive to Boston? Sometimes, being under pressure and having too many options makes it more difficult to make a decision.

What actually happened was that we did all three within a 36-hour period.

It was noon on November 12th, and Tracey, Nora and I were in the waiting area of the emergency room of the local hospital. We were already really frazzled with worry and indecision, still not sure that this was the best course of action. Tracey was wrestling with the admissions desk, as I helplessly sat in the waiting area holding little Nora while she was seizing every few minutes in my arms. There was absolutely nothing I could do about it. In the chair to my right sat an elderly gentlemen. He barely noticed Nora and certainly didn't notice the seizures; rather, he treated me as his captive audience, and as such poured out his own story and reason for being there in a lengthy monologue. His wife had taken ill. He rambled without taking a breath, adding heat to my already pressure-cooked feeling of anxiety. I wished I knew how to tell him to stop. I was fuming with anger. I wanted to say: *Hey, wake up stupid. You know what? You're old. That means you've had a lot of life, you've had time with your wife and options and choices and good times and bad times. You've lived your life for years and years. You've made it this far, be grateful. Wake up and look around you. Look at this poor baby who deserves the opportunities you've had. Be grateful and give some of the compassion you are looking for over here.*

I didn't say that, but I felt I needed to say something, where I once would have said nothing at all. When I finally spoke, it was from a different place. In an unexpected shift of perspective, I realized I needed to take my own advice. I needed to draw compassion from my own fear and anxiety. "I hope that you find out something soon and that everything will be alright," I said. As I did, I found myself on the other side of my anger and resentment. I hoped it helped him, I truly did.

As in most emergency room situations, you wait and wait and wait. This gave us much time to question this choice and the other options. The delay in admissions ultimately worked in our favor because Tracey and Glenn, who was on the phone, decided that we should bail out of this option and, as part of the new plan, take Nora upstairs to the blood lab to get her blood drawn. The rationale was that, regardless of where she went for treatment, her medication levels would be a key piece of information. Tracey began making the phone calls to get Boston to send the orders for Nora's blood draw. Some calls were lengthy, all of them frustrating. As she and Glenn finally sorted out the best solution, I tended to Nora. Again, I marveled at how helpful technology could be for us, realizing how much more impossible the situation would have been without a cell phone.

All the while, Nora's seizures persisted, exhausting her and straining our anxious feelings of helplessness. While waiting to be called for the blood draw, we moved to an empty waiting area near the lab, taking shelter in the privacy. By then, more than four hours had passed. We were tired, confused, and we felt powerless and scared. In a momentary lull, Nora finally dropped off to sleep in the stroller. The phone was silent, awaiting several important return calls. Around our heads, a cyclone of information, uncertainty and indecision swirled, and we stood in the vacuum of its eye, two mothers engulfed in tears, each sad and frustrated, being unable to rescue her daughter.

Of course, we had to wake Nora up for the blood draw and from there we drove to Connecticut Children's Medical Center , just 45 minutes away. Tracey called ahead to the doctors she'd talked with in the first few weeks of Nora's life. Having them involved in Nora's care going forward could be a real advantage, should there be some life-threatening emergency in the future. We arrived there around dinnertime and they were waiting for us. It was a relief to have that kind of reception.

After another six hours, two doses of sedatives, some relief for Nora, and much discussion with the doctors as to whether or not to admit her to the hospital, Tracey, Glenn and Nora went home.

The next day, Nora's seizures were not improved, so by evening, Nora, Tracey and I were on our way to Boston, driving in the dark of a torrential, raw November rainstorm. We had no idea how long we'd be in Boston. My attention was fragmented, thinking about Wade who was landing at the airport just as we were passing by it on the highway. He was returning from a remote area of Michigan where cell service was almost nonexistent. He had no idea what was going on, and would be surprised that it was my son and not me there to pick him up.

Of all the things I remember about this particular visit, foremost was how worn and weary Tracey was. Prior to this, many of the most serious decisions she faced were made while Nora was still in the safety of the hospital. This was the first episode of this nature outside the hospital. The increased seizures were disturbing enough, but why was this happening? What did it mean?

We were instructed to go directly to the emergency room in Boston to be admitted, even though the epilepsy doctors were expecting Nora's arrival up on the ninth floor. This was a re-admission and I remember being annoyed because, although Nora had been a patient there already and all her medications were being prescribed by their doctors, Tracey still had to provide Nora's entire medical history and every prescription to the nurse who was admitting Nora. It may have made precautionary sense, but rehashing each step of Nora's history was too much like having to relive it. With her two-inch ring binder notebook in hand, Tracey recited again, as she would many, many times after, the litany of Nora's growing medical text.

The emotion of that night is easy to recall, because it was captured in a photo. Believe it or not, we took lots of photos during those times, mostly with our cell phone cameras. I suppose that seems strange, to take photos of such events, when most people choose only to capture the happy times.

My father had been a news photographer. I grew up seeing tragic news photos, and my childhood was recorded in eight-by-ten, black-and-white photos. I found it strange when, in my adult years, I discovered photos he'd taken of my mother laid out at the funeral home. They were too painful for me to look at and I could never understand why he'd done it. Yet, there we were photographing all these weird and unhappy times with Nora. Was it a distraction, or did we do this because we could not grasp what was happening in the moment? Was that my father's reason, too? Did we actually intend to record these events for ourselves or for Nora? If the latter is true, then the photo I took is quintessential.

Like much of our time with Nora up to that point, the photo could be titled "Waiting." I took it while we were in a small holding room just outside the actual emergency room. It was almost midnight. Showing sympathy for our fatigue, the nurse had lowered the lights in the room before she left us. For that reason, the photo, like us, is fuzzy and grainy, with dark overtones. Tracey is sitting, with legs folded in a meditative-style pose on the gurney. Her back is against the wall. Just above her is a picture of colorful hot-air balloons; nearby the oxygen equipment is mounted, mask tucked away. She is dressed in what we'd come to call our hospital uniform: sneakers, sweatpants and an oversized sweatshirt. This day the pants are gray and the shirt is an orange fleece with "Tennessee" emblazoned on it. There is a hospital issue "Hello, my name is" sticker on the right-hand side of her shirt, which is there to identify her as the mother of the patient. She is looking down at Nora, who is cradled securely in her arms. Their gazes are locked. What I see in Nora's eyes, even at three months old, is a look of inquiry. Tracey's face expresses consternation over the all-too-many seizures she has been witnessing, and the anxious reflection of hours passed and of those to come; facing a future of dire uncertainty. In the moment and in the picture, I feel my daughter in her daughter … and I wonder, *how are we even doing this?*

Soon after, Nora was admitted and we were back on the familiar ninth floor. Based on the scheduled appointment, we were a week early, but Nora did have the MRI and the long-term monitoring as was intended. We ended up staying for almost a week, while the doctors worked on medications to stabilize Nora's seizures.

During this visit, Tracey adopted the hospital's blogging platform, called The Carepages, making it easy for her to communicate news to family and friends.

Carepages Post, Saturday, Nov. 15, 2008, 3:45PM

We have had so many discussions and are gathering so much information it can be difficult to summarize but all in all, we know we made the right decision in coming back to Boston when we did.

Nora's seizures, unfortunately, are still not under control, but the meds do take a few doses to kick in so she is being monitored closely and we'll see where she's at in a few days.

Earlier this afternoon, we did speak with the team of neurologists regarding Nora's EEG and I think we're all pleased to know that, so far, it appears that all seizures do seem to be originating from one area of her brain, which is the best we could hope for. This means that, if surgery is performed on that area, it has a high likelihood of being successful at stopping the seizures.

We were told the medical team would meet to evaluate her case while we were still in the hospital, but in actuality that meeting did not take place until after we were back home.

HARD TO SWALLOW

Carepages Post: Tuesday, Nov. 25, 2008, 7:31PM

Nora's case was reviewed among the doctors and surgeons at Boston Children's Hospital today and they have all collectively agreed that Nora is an excellent surgical candidate, which is good news. They also feel that surgery should happen sooner rather than later. This could mean surgery as early as within the next few weeks.

The malformation is quite extensive and the surgery would be very involved. There is much to consider. The news is bittersweet. Sweet, of course, because we know the surgery is the best opportunity we have to offer Nora the best quality of life. It is bitter, however, because we know there are serious risks involved in this type of surgery on such a little body.

We don't have information regarding dates and appointments as of yet, as Nora will need a few tests done in preparation and we'll need many questions answered, but we'll keep everyone posted as we learn more.

As you can imagine, this is a heart-wrenching time for us.

Happy Thanksgiving to everyone. Please be thankful for all of the healthy children born into your circle of life and please pray for those who may need a little extra something. May God bless you.

When December arrived, the idea of brain surgery for Nora loomed. We'd been back home for only two weeks and things had not been as calm as we had hoped.

Once again, I was sitting vigil, this time waiting for the sweep of headlights to wash the living room windows and signal my daughter's arrival and the news that she and my son-in-law would be bringing. Her text message just told me they were still 30 minutes away, yet my eyes darted to the window every 20 seconds or so, as though their arrival was imminent.

Nora was asleep in her portable crib a few feet away. I was still raw with empathy, feeling the 48-hour-old hole in her belly as if it were mine. My discomfort with the feeding tube portal that now filled the hole in her sweet, punctured belly had at least replaced the greater fear of her dehydration, which had necessitated the surgery. This all within the past 72 hours.

We had been waiting for Nora's new combination of medications to take effect. This time, her reaction to the change greatly impacted her alertness and appetite.

There had also been concerns about the efficiency of Nora's ability to swallow. A test result seemed to indicate that she might be aspirating, meaning that when swallowing, food might be going into her lungs. We were somewhat skeptical about the findings, because she had been crying hysterically during the test, known as a barium swallow study. The procedure forced her, at three months old, to attempt to ingest barium off of a spoon. Due to her age and her medical challenges, she was not capable of that or able to sit upright as was required. Forcing the spoon of gook and holding her in an upright position, while attempting to extend her little neck so as to X-ray her throat at the exact moment of swallowing, was ludicrous. Regardless of the idiocy of that test for her and the findings from it, her safety could not be ignored.

After the test results, we became diligent about her position while feeding, keeping her head higher than her chest, her chin up and her neck in a straight line. We listened carefully to her swallows and breathing as she sucked on the bottle.

With the most recent change in her medications, she became listless and uninterested in eating, so much so that it had gotten almost impossible to get her to suck on the bottle. She was too drugged to eat, but if she didn't eat we couldn't get the drugs into her. The whole process just worked against itself and her. The most imminent danger was the most fundamental: dehydration, which for babies can happen in mere hours and be fatal. The fear of it sent us all to Connecticut Children's Medical Center for another five days, this time for Nora to have surgery to implant a feeding tube in her stomach.

Once again, Nora was challenging us to learn skills we'd never wanted to know. By the time we left the hospital just that morning, despite my trepidation and clumsy nature, I could adequately perform the 15-step tube-feeding and medication-delivery process. Like many other things since Nora's birth, I found this almost impossible to believe. I was proud of myself for being able to overcome my squeamishness, striving to master the process in the hospital while I had nurses at my elbow. It turned out to be a good decision, because upon her discharge, I had driven Nora back home to my house for the day; while her parents drove off in the opposite direction to keep their appointment with Dr. Madsen, the neurosurgeon, in Boston.

The surgery they would be discussing is called a hemispherectomy. For patients like Nora, whose seizures are "intractable," which means they cannot be controlled by medications, sometimes surgery can be a solution. Generally, surgery is only performed if the neurologists and neurosurgeons are convinced that the seizures are coming from one location in the brain.

The operation would involve identifying the problem area, in Nora's case the malformation, and disconnecting and sometimes removing that part of abnormal brain. Success rates for these procedures vary considerably, depending on the specific disease, the origination and localization of seizures and the patient's particular medical situation. .

I was surprised to learn that the first hemispherectomy was performed in the 1930s and, after many unsuccessful outcomes the procedure fell into disfavor, mainly due to the then-nearly inevitable post-surgical complications, which included excessive bleeding, infection and problems with the cavity left behind. In the 1980s, Dr. Ben Carson, renowned neurosurgeon and author of *Gifted Hands* and five other best-selling books, resurrected the procedure while at Johns Hopkins Hospital. Believing that the post-surgical complications that once were a threat would be less of an issue because of modern medical advances, he studied and then performed the operation first in an attempt to relieve the seizures and reclaim the quality of life for a four-year-old girl who was experiencing 120 seizures a day. The surgery was a success. Carson went on and, among other successful brain surgeries, separated twins who were conjoined at the back of the head. Had he not taken on the challenge of revisiting this brain surgery, it's likely that Nora would not have even the possibility of a life without seizures.

The hemispherectomy requires the patient to be under general anesthetic. The surgeon makes an incision in the scalp, removes a piece of bone and pulls back a section of the dura, which is the tough membrane that covers the brain. Through this opening, the surgeon utilizes special instruments and surgical microscopes, which provide a magnified view of the brain's structure. During the procedure, the surgeon may remove portions of the affected hemisphere, often taking all of the temporal lobe but leaving the frontal and parietal lobes. The surgeon also gently separates the hemispheres to access and cut the corpus callosum, which is the "bridge" between the two hemispheres. After the tissue is removed, the dura and bone are put back into place, and the scalp is closed using stitches or staples.

Not surprisingly, the patient loses the functionality controlled by that half of the brain. The loss of function is greatest if the hemisphere being removed has normal or near-normal function to begin with. That half of Nora's brain was not functional, so losing it would likely be less noticeable, but the outcome would be impossible to predict. The sooner the surgery was performed, the more transfer of functionality could occur, due to her brain's ability to create new neural pathways that have the potential to restore lost functionality.

Choosing carefully from among the excellent neurosurgeons that could do the surgery, Tracey and Glenn selected Dr. Joseph Madsen at Boston Children's Hospital. Of the physicians on Nora's team, it was he who would provide the most input at the meeting we were waiting to hear about.

When Tracey and Glenn finally arrived, they looked as drained as one could expect, given the events of the days prior.

Wade and I were silent as they reported the details of the meeting. My attention bounced between listening and attempting to read their faces and body language.

When considering the possibility of surgery early on, the surgeon had wanted Nora to grow as much as possible to lessen the risks, which still included undue blood loss and post-surgical infection. It would be a long surgery for such a little child. He'd hoped to wait, but it now seemed so necessary to go forward. Indications were that Nora might actually be the youngest child to ever undergo the surgery, at least at that hospital.

"Dr. Madsen feels a functional hemispherectomy, as opposed to an anatomical hemispherectomy, is the best course of action for Nora," said Tracey.

"What's the difference?" I asked. I still couldn't fathom that the answer really had anything to do with Nora. I wasn't sure if I expected her answer to make me feel any better about the whole thing.

"An anatomical hemispherectomy is when they remove half of the brain. A functional hemispherectomy entails just disconnecting the two sides without removing the malfunctioning side. Both operations stop communication between the two hemispheres, which prevents the impulses that cause the seizures from traveling from one side of the brain to the other. Dr. Madsen feels that all the tests show that Nora's seizures are coming from the left side of her brain, so chances of stopping the seizures are very good. He's leaning toward the functional hemispherectomy for Nora, because it typically means less blood loss and often fewer post-surgical problems."

Her last words hung in the air with such disturbing resonance. It was suddenly becoming all too real, and the realization rendered us speechless. We all looked over at Nora, so peacefully asleep.

Tracey broke the silence, "He did say that performing this surgery on someone as young as Nora is far from ideal, but he can see the benefits of providing her with a better quality of life … hopefully seizure-free, as soon as possible." Her eyes and mine were full of tears. Wade and I were still dumbfounded, at a total loss for words.

"We asked him," "Glenn offered, "if he had to make this choice for his own child, what he would do. He said, without hesitation, that if this were his child there would be no question that he would opt for the surgery." From dad to dad, I felt that meant a lot to them, regardless of how much they feared the surgery. I could tell they felt confident about their choice of surgeon.

"It's hard to say what else might be affected," said Tracey. "Because it's her left hemisphere, there could be problems with speech; it's hard to tell. They definitely say that she would lose some vision on the right side, at least peripheral vision. The rest is unknown. The good thing is that she's young and the brain is what they call "plastic." It can remap functionality to the other side of her brain with the help of therapy. There is concern that the remapping would displace or overcrowd the working side of her brain. There is just no way to know in advance. The important thing is to stop the seizures.

"Dr. Madsen wants to hold off as long as possible. He does have a spot in his schedule before Christmas. He just did the surgery on a little boy who was six months old. Nora will be younger. Again, waiting until she's older would be better. Anyway, when it does happen, the surgery is expected to last about eight hours. If at any point he feels there are complications, he has a very clear plan for how to safely stop the operation, which is helpful to know. He admits that technological advances over the past five years have made this surgery relatively safe to perform on little ones."

How Tracey and Glenn were still standing, having just made the trip from one hospital to the other, from one surgery to a discussion of another, and then the two-and-a-half hour drive home so late in the evening, was impossible for me to imagine.

With too much to ponder and nothing left to say, they bundled little Nora into her carrier. Tracey and I went on to practical discussions of schedules and plans for the rest of the week, and life moved on as unusually as it had for the past few months.

CHRISTMAS

Soon after the meeting with the surgeon, the date for Nora's brain surgery was set for January 16th. Now we were facing the Christmas season, as if anyone felt like celebrating. Christmas time is always difficult for me, even in the best of years. I know I am not alone in that. The true spirit left me in 1960, the year my mother died. That year, the holiday came a mere three months after my mother's death. Knowing that my father was overwhelmed by having been recently widowed and left to figure out how to deal on his own with four children, ages two-and-a-half to sixteen, our neighbors thoughtfully shopped for and wrapped an array of gifts for us. Christmas morning 1960, the floor beneath our tree was filled with presents that did little more than leave an even emptier feeling in me. Without my mother, they meant nothing. They were just things that reminded me that she was gone. I could never look at even one of them without being reminded that she had not chosen it for me.

That was also the last Christmas in our house. During the year prior to my mother's death, my parents had been searching the religious landscape for something more meaningful than our Lutheran church offered them. We had stopped going to our church and strangers began visiting our home. They sat in our living room and talked with my parents for hours at a time. The rise and fall and the tone of their voices let even a child know that the subject was serious. Several times our family went to religious gatherings that were not held in a church. I later learned the people at these gatherings were Jehovah's Witnesses. There was tension in our house around these events, but I didn't know why. Years later, I discovered that my mother did not agree with their teachings, but my father did.

After my mother's death, my father eventually left that organization, but he went on to others, leading us along through his quest for the "truth." He ultimately embraced his own version of beliefs that eliminated Christmas and most major holidays altogether from our home. Easter was one holiday we celebrated, but the Easter Bunny was nowhere to be found in it. Even our birthdays were eliminated.

I believed then that my father truly wanted to save my soul. The fact that I knew this and that I didn't think he meant to be cruel still didn't make it any easier to live with. I knew his beliefs were strong and he was steadfast in them. It was not until years after his death that I learned how strong. I discovered that because of the dictates of the religion he was following, he refused to authorize a blood transfusion for my mother. A surgical error caused her to lose excessive amounts of blood and she ultimately died of blood loss. His beliefs very likely cost my 38-year-old mother her life. I know my father dearly loved my mother—she was the center of his life. I cannot imagine how he or anyone could make that decision. I know he must have suffered from it afterwards. I know we did.

When I got married, I began celebrating Christmas with my husband and then my children, without observing the religious underpinnings, but it always causes me anxiety because it never feels like enough. Regardless of what I do, I can't recapture the feeling. Unlike me, my sister loves all things Christmas; every aspect of it. She loves all the symbolism, the decorations, sparkles, colors, gifts, and most of all, family gatherings. And unlike me, she embraces religion wholeheartedly and is active in her faith of her choice.

In 2008, the year Nora was born, my sister came from Tennessee to Connecticut to spend the holidays with us. She was driving a friend to Pennsylvania, and drove on to us.

I looked forward to her Christmas energy, as my mood continued to be challenged by Christmases past and the present-day situation. I did my best to muster some enthusiasm for the holiday, though we didn't put up a tree; instead we decorated the house outside with lights.

Once again, Nora's seizures were continuing at a rate too frequent to ignore. If things didn't improve, Tracey, Nora and I would be heading up to Boston again. Christmas was only five days away. If we went, chances were we'd have to celebrate the holiday there.

My sister came down with the flu as she arrived at her friend's house midway, and was forced to stay there for a few days until she recovered.

In the meantime, Nora rallied a little with changes to her meds.

My sister finally arrived on Christmas Eve, a scant few hours before dinner. She would finally be able to meet Nora. As their Aunt, my sister had been a big part of my children's lives when they were growing up. I knew Tracey was excited to see her, too. It felt like it would be a good Christmas after all.

In the kitchen, while we were cooking Christmas Eve dinner, my sister and I talked about Tracey and Nora.

"I don't know how you do it," she said about my intense involvement and hospital stays. "How could I not? I wish I could do more, and it always makes me feel better to be with them. I can't explain it, but I somehow think that Nora is the reason I was born."

The last sentence surprised me, as it seemed to come from nowhere; no forethought, either momentary or otherwise, had prompted it. It just came out and, for me, it rang with the resonance of truth. Busy with the tasks at hand, I tucked it away for future consideration.

Tracey and her family arrived a few hours later.

Nora was adorable in her red velvet Santa dress. It was clear that her seizures were escalating again. It was startling and dismaying what a difference one day could make with them. We had just hoped to have a good Christmas. If only the damned seizures could have held off one more day. We were only 20 days away from Nora's surgery and we had hoped those days could be spent enjoying the holidays and resting up at home. It wasn't looking good, but it made us aware that we needed to be grateful for what we did have; that Nora was with us. With that, we shook off the shadow of her illness and celebrated. Photos of that night are some of my favorites.

By the time the 26th dawned, Tracey had contracted a mild bout of the flu and Glenn came down with it later that day. His was much worse.

By the 27th, Nora, Tracey, and I were traveling to Boston for another round of seizure control, leaving my sister behind to fend for herself. Graciously, Wade would be host for her stay until we returned. Sadly though, by the time we arrived in Boston, he had come down with the flu that left him incapacitated for three full days. Some holiday! I felt awful having to leave my sister, and this was just a mess for both of them.

Tracey, Nora and I had made so many trips to Boston for checkups, seizure control and overnight tests that we'd become adept at packing and traveling. By now we had become a well-oiled machine, knowing how to live and function in the hospital environment. Everything was familiar and felt safe. Tracey and I agreed again that, even though we were reluctant to acknowledge it, going to Boston Children's Hospital felt a bit like going home. It was familiar and the safest place on the planet for us. The staff cared, understood, and either helped or were trying to help Nora. When we were there among others like us, we were normal. We fit in because we shared something unspoken with those around us. In this cocoon, we all rode the same crazy rollercoaster. Even in the elevator, shoulder-to-shoulder with strangers, we felt as if we were among family. Everyone there had a child or loved a child or was helping a child endure illness or get well.

The hospital environment is never pleasant, but one becomes accustomed to it. The routine was predictable. Even surprises were familiar. Under the circumstances, two comforting things prevailed: the first was that in contrast to the many demands of life, here we had a singular focus and we felt much safer there than at home. We always had to endure the pain of watching Nora have seizures, but with expert staff at our elbows we were doing all we possibly could for her.

On this visit 9 North was, for the most part, empty. Scheduled surgeries were fewer during the holidays, as were elective long-term monitoring patients. Because of this, we were given a double room, which allowed the three of us to all stay overnight together right there. This eliminated some expenses and just made things easier for us. During our stay, I think there was only one night that either of us left the building. Tracey was suffering what we surmised was severe indigestion, and I left the hospital to get some over-the-counter antacid medicine. Seemed silly but, if you aren't a patient, the staff can't give you as much as an aspirin.

Also during this visit, we experienced a full 16 hours in which Nora had no seizures at all. Our lightened mood, in contrast to many other visits, made that part of the trip feel more like a pajama party than a hospital visit. As soon as we started thinking we could pack for home, Nora's seizures returned in full force. On the morning of New Year's Eve we were greeted with a snow storm. It looked as though we'd be staying. The thought of greeting a new year in the hospital was not the tone we wanted to set for the coming year, though we were well aware of the huge part it was about to play in our future.

It just so happened that the little boy who had had the hemispherectomy surgery at six months old had been admitted and was on our floor, too. Tracey had been given the contact information of several families whose children had gone through the surgery, and had spoken to the boy's father on the phone, but had never met either parent. Now they were just down the corridor from us. William had undergone this surgery just six weeks prior. He was back in the hospital with an illness that kept us out of his room, but we hoped we could visit before we left.

Carepages Post, December 31, 2008, 11:20AM

Today's report from Boston is that Nora had a fairly good night and her seizures seem to be a little bit less frequent, which is no doubt a result of the medication changes we've been making. Mom and I would be ready to take her home today and continue to work on medication shifts at home. However, the snow has us staying put at least for the rest of the day. If we're lucky and it clears out late this afternoon, we may head home after dinner. We're playing it by ear ... which seems to be the theme of all things Nora Jane. We'd love to be back home with the family, but don't want to risk getting stuck in snowy traffic jams all the way home.

Happy New Year to all! May 2009 bring you peace, joy, and prosperity.

In the early evening, the snowstorm was all but over, Nora's seizures were finally more controlled, and the doctors cleared us to leave. As we were packing, Tracey was given permission to visit the boy down the hall. It turned out he wasn't contagious, making it fine to visit. This was the first time that Tracey could actually meet another mother who really knew what she was facing.

I let her go on alone to meet them. I stayed with Nora and finished packing. Then, with Nora in arms, I ventured down the hall to find Tracey. I was hungry to see little William. He was blissfully asleep in the crib. Seeing the huge crescent scar on the side of his head made me ache, but it was also strangely comforting that now, just six weeks after surgery, it was so well healed that it looked like someone had drawn a red crescent on his head with a medium-point felt-tipped marker. At that moment, I chose to avoid thinking about the fact that, just before the scar was made, someone probably had.

We took our time driving home on snowy roads and made it just before the New Year arrived. That felt like a really good omen.

GETTING READY

Regardless of what was happening at each moment, the big red X on the calendar on January 16th was the mountain we were preparing to climb without really knowing what was on the other side. Preparation meant clearing our calendars, and packing and thinking ahead about all our needs for ten full days. Lodging and ten days of meals for three adults isn't part of any health insurance package. Tracey put out the call for assistance and tapped into all the hospital resources she could find. Helpful family and friends responded to the call by cooking and freezing meals for us to take. We also obtained pre-paid meal vouchers for the hospital café and for nearby restaurants.

I prepared by finishing up any work I had before we left. A few months earlier, I had acquired a new client. The first project I undertook for this client had been very successful. The deadline on the second project was the week before surgery. I pushed to finish and clear my calendar, but delays at the client's end kept things from being finalized. A few days before the surgery, they threw me a curve ball, insisting on a whole new direction and a plan that would require delivery of the writing the following week. The deadline collided with the surgery schedule. I didn't think I could finish before I left. I broke my personal privacy rule and shared my situation with the marketing manager, explaining that I would not be working during that time. I hoped it would convince her to cut me some slack. It didn't. I worked furiously until we left for Boston, but there was still more to do.

Wade and I drove to Boston the night before surgery. Though I had driven the route to Boston several times alone, this night I got us lost, even with the aid of the GPS. I was anxious and my nerves so frazzled that the frustration of getting lost made me explosive. It was just one of the many times for which Wade deserves a medal for putting up with me.

When we did finally get there, we went directly to the hospital housing where Tracey, Glenn, and Nora were staying. That evening Nora was as sweet as ever, seemingly unaffected by the stress we were striving to contain. I remember that Tracey let me be the one to hold Nora for her last feeding of the night, the last feeding before surgery. I sat on the edge of the bed holding her, cherishing every ounce of her, not allowing myself to think where she'd be or who she'd be the following night.

When Wade and I got to our hotel room a few miles away, attempting to sleep was even more impossible than I had anticipated. Our hotel room was dreadful. It reeked of cigarette smoke from smokers in an adjoining room. It was already quite late and we were too worn out to complain or change rooms.

ENDURANCE

Although it was still dark, it wasn't difficult to rise at 4:30 a.m. We had gotten little sleep, if any. A day of emotional conflict was dawning. I had wondered and also had avoided wondering about this day through the days and sleepless nights leading up to it, anticipating the possibilities it held. And now, I dreaded, dreaded, dreaded the next 24 hours. We traveled the few miles between hotel and hospital in pitch darkness. Text messages exchanged with Tracey kept us connected. Our lives were about to change, but how?

We met the three of them in the hospital's pre-op waiting room. It was only 5:30 a.m., but the large, brightly decorated waiting room was buzzing with activity as if it was midday.

Two concentric circles of seats were nearly filled with other families, with children of all ages. Some of the children were pajama-clad and oblivious, others cried and clung, while some of the older ones were silent, but clearly frightened.

There was an air of camaraderie among the caregivers. We might never actually converse, yet we knowingly all shared the anxiety of waiting for our patient's name to be called. Every few minutes a few chairs in the room would empty, as patient and entourage moved on in the process.

It was no surprise that Tracey, Glenn, Wade, and I looked as awful as we felt. Nora-the-beautiful slept, cradled in the arms of her father, her pacifier tethered to her brightly colored polka-dotted pajamas. Had we been waiting in an adult pre-op space, as opposed to a children's hospital, anyone would have assumed from Glenn's face and body language that he was the patient-to-be and in great physical pain. I am sure that he was.

I was careful to remain captive in the moment, appreciating the second-to-second luxury of not yet having to take the next step or withstand the next barrage of feeling.

"Nora Blackman?" The call came, leaving the echo of her name hanging, like my stomach, in midair.

We scrambled to grab our piles of belongings with the kind of clumsy confusion that reminded me of Nora's helicopter transport day; the sort of flurry that ensues when anticipation collides with reluctant action. We were all escorted to the bank of elevators. Wade and I would go directly to the surgical floor waiting area. Nora, Tracey and Glenn would go on to pre-op. Before entering the elevator, I stroked Nora's little head and kissed her cheek. There was nothing more to do, nothing to say except, "I love you; see you later."

When we arrived in the waiting area, it looked different than the way it had been described to me. No windows, no sofas, no food cart. We quickly discovered that we had found the outpatient waiting area. Walking deeper into the space, we recognized it; the "marathon waiting area." In contrast to the stark, outpatient section, this space communicated a "make-your-self-comfortable-it's-going-to-be-a-long-day" aesthetic.

The waiting room was at least 75 feet long, rectangular and carpeted. It was bright, without trying to be too cheery. Huge banks of floor-to-ceiling windows lined the right-hand side and cornered with the back wall at the far end. Set against the windows were eight to ten small seating areas, consisting of a small coffee table, a sofa and several stuffed armchair/beds like those I'd slept on when staying overnight in Nora's hospital room.

Outside, the morning's light was just crowning above the building tops, but not yet reaching down to the streets below.

We were the second of the patient entourages to arrive in this waiting area. Wade and I surveyed the scene, having many choices from which to select as our "camp" for the day. As if there could be a perfect spot, we hesitated here and there and then settled at the end, into the seating area farthest from the room's entry point. We rearranged the chairs we'd need, including one of the sleeper models. Making certain there were nearby electrical outlets for laptops, we settled in. Already it seemed we had been there forever. I dared not try to imagine in any detail what was happening on the surgical floor.

I cannot recall any other time in my life that came close to instilling the kind of fear I was feeling. At five months and three days old, Nora was one of the youngest patients to undergo this surgery. We were fortunate that she was otherwise healthy.

In addition to the dangers and complications of other types of surgeries, it seemed to me that with brain surgery came greater concerns about what could be affected, impaired, or totally lost in the process. The question of who Nora would be afterward gnawed at me.

At least 90 minutes had passed since we had arrived. The waiting area was nearly full. After having looked up for the two-hundredth time from the book I was pretending to read, I finally saw Tracey and Glenn walking toward us. Their eyes were downcast. I vacillated between watching them and turning my eyes elsewhere. I imagined they would prefer not to be scrutinized. When I finally embraced Tracey, I couldn't speak. What could I possibly say? We simply shared tears. "I'll be alright ..." she said, "eventually."

"She did fine," they offered, describing events in the pre-op process. "When we left she was asleep." With that, one of my personal terrors abated, having been an emotional victim of an unnatural act of mother/child separation. The demons of my childhood, when exhumed, still evoke such strong feelings that the thought of leaving Nora awake among only strangers was one I could not bear. In telling the story of this day, I feel guilty admitting the intensity of the fear I felt and I never mean to imply that it was more difficult or devastating for me than for Nora's parents. It was different and certainly magnified by the duality of my relationships as mother and grandmother. But secretly I was also terrified, albeit selfishly that, should the worst happen, in addition to everything else, I simply could not endure the loss of the inexplicable connection I had been gifted with in Nora.

We all did our best to settle down in the waiting area. For me, that meant trying to make the best of sitting on pins and needles. Looking back, the day is a blur and I can recount only certain moments and incidents, but I do remember that, of the more than seven hundred and eighty minutes that passed, I missed not one. Never once did I look at the clock and think, *that went by fast.* Instead, as nervous time-checking increased, so did the time drag.

There were events. Every 90 minutes, a woman—I called her, "The Patient Ambassador" appeared, armed with a clipboard and a pleasant yet poker face *(was that part of the job description?).* The clipboard held a status sheet. She would make her way through the room, stopping at each family to update them on the progress of their patient's surgery. These updates came to be a strange drug for me. Watching this woman make her way toward us, stopping at the other "camps" took at least ten minutes. It was as nerve-jangling as I could imagine waiting for a fix would be to a drug addict. Unfortunately, these fixes brought no real relief. It seemed we waited and waited, and the progression of events as reported was painfully slow, and I feared not particularly true.

9:30 a.m.: "The anesthesia is underway, the draping is being placed and the surgery will begin shortly. Next update at 10:45 a.m. or so," she said.

It was actually closer to 11 a.m. by the time she got to us. "Not much to tell, they're doing very, very well. Nora is nice and stable and they're working on getting to the spot they need to reach. It's a slow process and everything is fine," she said.

1:00 p.m.: "The surgery is going well. Nora continues to be nice and stable and the blood loss is normal. They have accessed the area they need to and things are okay. The doctor is taking a short break."

Weeks before the surgery, Tracey had received information and gifts from The Hemispherectomy Foundation, an internationally-known nonprofit organization dedicated to helping children and families impacted by this brain surgery. Kristi and Cris Hall founded the organization after having gone through the experience with their own daughter.

There was also a similarly-inspired Massachusetts-based organization, The Tyler Foundation, founded by Tyler's parents, Heather and Eric Plotkin whose mission was to offer aid to families of "hemi" children.

Eric had taken time on his lunch hour that day to visit us at the hospital, bringing us thoughtful gifts, supplies, parking and food vouchers, and restaurant gift cards that knowingly addressed our needs. He was one of us; he knew how we felt, which was comforting.

3:00 p.m.: "She's lost a good deal of blood. It is to be expected. Things are progressing." By this time of day, more than half of the other waiting families and been escorted to the recovery area to be reunited with their children.

The afternoon wore on and, despite the huge windows, the sun's slanted winter rays intersected by neighboring buildings never reached in with any warmth. We were now at almost the eight-hour mark, the anticipated length of the ordeal, yet there was no indication of an end in sight from the "still working" reports.

The winter daylight had begun receding, taking with it some of the patience and stoic resolve we had stockpiled. We felt the same vulnerability one comes to know when facing overly long exposure to the punishing elements of nature. It was much like a feeling of being stranded in the middle of the ocean; this was the eerie feeling of being left behind, as we were now one of only two families left waiting in the expansive space. In fact, the other family was actually part of a second wave of families to come through much later in the day.

The last thing I expected or wanted to see was Nora's surgeon approaching us. My heart stopped. Shouldn't he be in surgery with her? They hadn't told us the surgery was winding down. Clearly, this wasn't supposed to happen. It could not be good.

Watching him make his way from the far end of the long room took far too much time, leaving too much time for me to think. I fixated on his body language, giving attention to his overall demeanor until he got close enough for me to study his face. It didn't bode well. We all remained seated. He stood outside our circle of chairs, standing directly across from mine. When he began speaking, he adopted a storytelling style of rhetoric, recounting past conversations he'd had with Tracey and Glenn, reiterating old information as one might do if wanting to avoid the present situation. I was vibrating with anxiety from my fears. My inner voice was screaming, *get to the point.*

"She's lost a lot of blood," he said. "We did discuss that was a concern." My fear was taking flight. "She's had more transfusions than I'd hoped"... blah blah ... "blood clot ..." he continued.

What?! What is he saying, what is he trying to tell us? I began to feel intense heat and hear the white noise that signals I am about to lose consciousness. I gently slid myself down from my chair to the floor so that, if I passed out, I wouldn't fall. I was glad no one noticed, they were all looking at him.

A clot on her brain? Oh, my God, what is he trying to tell us? What does this mean? I didn't want to go the places my mind was taking me. *Is she gone? Is she brain-dead?* My fear was in full grip, which quickly gave way to the throes of white-hot anger. I wanted to grab the surgeon and shake him: *oh, please, get to the point.*

It seemed much longer, but within a minute or two he revealed that Nora had lost more blood than expected. She had been given more than the anticipated number of transfusions until it became unwise to continue. Though he had only accomplished 75% of the surgery; it was not safe to go on. He would close, see how things went, and if necessary at some point in the future, they could discuss completing the surgery. Because he was concerned about swelling and pressure on her brain, he would not be reattaching the piece of bone—he called it a bone flap—that he had removed from Nora's head to do the surgery.

What does THAT mean? Tracey and Glenn asked all the right questions. It sounded scary, but it was secondary. We could deal with that later.

Okay, but wait, I get that but, did he say blood clot? Did he say at the top of her brain, or something like that?

"She will be closely monitored," he added.

Blood clot—did anyone else get that? Did anyone else hear that he said that? Isn't that really serious, especially in the brain? He seems not to be emphasizing it. Should I ask?

As I often do, I doubted myself. I thought maybe the stress made it all too much for me to grasp. I pulled back and simply observed. Tracey and Glenn had begun asking other questions. They remained seemingly calm, and it was then that the surgeon crouched down to put himself at eye-level with us. I interpreted this to mean that he no longer feared our reaction to the news.

Tracey and Glenn both looked confused, worn out and concerned, but the expression on their faces was not aligned with what I felt about what I thought I had heard. While I still doubted my understanding, I swore I could feel something uneasy in the surgeon's demeanor. Was there more? Without doubt, I sensed some residual uneasiness from him. This was a decision point: Should I clarify? At this point, what would it do for us? I did not ask for clarification, nor did I make my fears and feelings known. There was nothing to know, or nothing we hadn't already thought about and faced. There were no decisions to be made. We would have to wait for time to reveal the answers. I felt absolutely no relief; in fact, I felt worse.

When the surgeon went back to Nora, he left us with disappointment. The milestone of hope that this could all be over was now again pushed back to the horizon. And from where we were, even the feeling of relief at the surgery portion of the day being over was still three hours away. It would be at least that long until Nora would be brought up to the Intensive Care Unit where we could see her. We had three hours to sit with what we had heard.

Darkness came.

We were still there waiting at 8:00 p.m., the only ones left in the too empty, too quiet and cavernous waiting area. It was closing time there and we were ushered out and left to wait briefly in a small consultation room just around the corner until we could go up to the ICU. Nora's epilepsy doctor paid us a visit. Her familiar face and her soft Irish brogue were soothing, and I gratefully allowed her words to wash over me. I thought I saw something in her eyes that seemed to confirm what I thought I'd heard. It made me believe all the more that there was something more serious, something more at stake now than Nora's seizures.

Sometime between 8:30 p.m. and 9:30 p.m. we were finally taken up to the Intensive Care floor to be reunited with Nora. Tracey and Glenn went in. Wade and I were left in the hallway outside the ICU. I had been holding back my fears of the seriousness of the surgeon's meanings for three hours; now I unleashed them on Wade. Had he heard it the way I had?

"He said something about a blood clot. That she'd lost a lot of blood, yes, but he also said something about a blood clot. Did you hear him say that?" I asked.

He hadn't.

"He passed over it lightly, but he said it. He said that they'd be monitoring it closely, or something like that. I think this is serious, Wade; this is really, really serious. I think we could lose her," I said.

Among the host of fears leading up to this point, a new one surfaced. What if … what's left is not Nora? Standing again, like the day she was born, in some strange hospital hallway, I didn't know what to do… Again the answer was … there's nothing you can do. Just wait.

Intensive care in a children's hospital is a heart-wrenching place. The atmosphere is as intense as can be imagined. By the time Wade and I were allowed into the restricted ICU area, the hallway's lighting had been dimmed for the night. We were able only to stand outside the large sliding glass door that separated Nora's room from the hallway. Her room was crammed with machines, monitors and people tending to them and Nora. I couldn't see her, but I could see Tracey and Glenn standing as close as they could get to the white metal crib in the center of the room, looking like two chess pieces out of place. Their body language was telling the story of torture I could feel.

Finally a path cleared and we could see Nora clearly. I had braced myself, expecting to be frightened by what I might see, but I was so hungry for a look at her that just to see her at all was a relief. Her face was very pale. She still looked like our Nora, except that the left side of her head was covered by a large bandage. And I could not count the number of wires and tubes that extended out in all directions from her body, making our past equipment-tethering experiences pale in comparison. The one I most hated was the breathing tube in her mouth. But at that moment, from where I stood, I couldn't see the tubes coming out of the top of her head. As if all of this wasn't enough, there was the handwritten sign taped to the crib above her head that said: "NO BONE IN LEFT SIDE OF HEAD."

I decided not to allow myself to think about that or anything else; that would be the best way to avoid my panic. There was a lot of activity in and around Nora's room, and I needed relief from it all. I stepped back and away from the door. Directly behind me, across from Nora's door was the main nurses' station for the floor. Was this a coincidence?

I ended up with my back almost touching the nurses' station counter. I turned to see two nurses behind it, watching the action. Our eyes met and I told them, "I am her grandmother." I thought once again I saw some veiled look cross their faces. I felt somehow they knew something that they wouldn't voice. They did mention that Nora had lost a lot of blood, but didn't go any further. Again, I thought I detected feeling that I was right about what I had heard. It could be really serious.

When Wade and I were able to go to Nora's crib side, we made our visit very brief. Even though she lay there without any covering or blanket, finding a place to touch her skin was difficult because of all the devices attached to her. I found and touched an area on her right leg. She felt very cool to me. I couldn't forget that my mother died of blood loss and I remembered, though I did not want to, what I had overheard my father say about the night my mother died. When he was with her in the recovery room, she kept asking for a blanket, complaining that she was cold.

I avoided thinking by suppressing my thoughts, and stood there trying to squeeze into the void between each breath I took, being grateful that we were at least on this end of this day.

Bodies wear out under stress. All four of us felt drained, with no transfusion in sight. We needed food and a break. It seemed strange and scary to leave her, but at the same time it was clear that Nora was getting excellent attention and care. We could best serve her by fortifying ourselves for the coming hours and days. We would head back to the hospital housing for some of the home-cooked food we had brought with us. Wishing I could rise to the moment, but feeling utterly depleted of energy, I was grateful that Glenn wanted to stay that night in Nora's room.

It was 10:30 p.m. when we started out on the four-block walk from the hospital to the house. As if we had not already staved off enough stress, it was the most brutally cold night, even for January. The 30-mile-an-hour winds were punishing. Our coats and hats were as defenseless against the elements as we were against the emotional maelstrom of the day. As we walked, I felt each step I took was one more than I thought I could take.

TEN DAYS

The first five post-surgical days were torturous.

Wade and I had spent the night after surgery in the room in hospital housing. Glenn had stayed with Nora, and Tracey slept in the parents' quarters in the hospital. The morning following the surgery, Wade left for home and I arrived back at the hospital at just about 8:30 a.m. I was anxious.

The ICU was as different a world from any other we'd been in with Nora. Here the doors to the room were huge, double, sliding glass doors designed to make the swift entry and exit of beds and equipment easier. Rather than the beds being placed perpendicular to the doorway, they were vertically aligned to it so that, if the privacy curtains were not closed, the patient could be easily seen from the hallway. For that reason, it was impossible to walk through the hallways and not catch sight of the children in other rooms. As sad as this was, I was always thankful that all of them could have such expert care. I never took that for granted. In all Nora and her parents endured, I was always mindful of our good fortune in living in the United States, not in some third-world country, where we would most likely have had to helplessly watch Nora endure seizure after seizure, with no real possibility of relief.

In the corridors of the ICU, between every two rooms, nurses' posts were strategically placed, allowing them to have a full view of each of the two patients' rooms at all times. This was so that children were never left unattended.

Though I'd been here the night before, this was really the first time I was consciously entering the room in full awareness of the surroundings. Being confronted by Nora's crib as I entered the room caught me off-guard, as my eyes were fully on her before I had anticipated it. Regardless, I could not have been prepared for what I saw. We'd been told to expect swelling, but did not anticipate that Nora's thin, angelic face would be swollen to proportions that now made it nearly as wide as it was high. Her once slender fingers were puffy; her legs and arms looked as if she'd gained ten pounds overnight. Waves of anguish washed over me. This was one of the moments I had been dreading, except it wasn't a moment. It didn't stop when I looked away and looked back. True, we were on this side of the surgery. Only in that way did I feel better than yesterday.

In the daylight, it was now easy to see the entire room and all of the medical equipment around her. There were bags hanging above the bed that were connected to pumps that were connected to tubes pumping fluids in, and tubes connected to pumps that were pumping fluids out into other bags. Stretching across her face, above, below and on the right side of her mouth were strips of tape, placed there to hold the breathing tube in her mouth. Connected to this was a tangle of tubes and wires leading to a machine dedicated to monitoring airflow and quality. Nora's arms were incapacitated--the right one splinted for the IV, the left one wrapped and restrained to keep her from being able to touch her own head. There were literally wires and tubes attached and running every which way from and around her in the bed. A quick count indicated 21 before confusion made me give up counting. She was ensnared in a miraculous but ugly web.

Nora was totally sedated. I could not have been more thankful for that. Her head was oddly bandaged, only on the left side. I would have expected a full turban. Small shadowy smears of darkness, dried blood and orange disinfectant hinted at yesterday's horror. Her left ear was at an almost 45 degree angle to her head. Her nose was the only part of her face that was somewhat familiar.

Glenn was up and about and talking with the nurse. He looked disheveled and tired; what else could he have been? What I had come to love and appreciate was his ability to engage in a kind of cavalier banter that could elevate the mood above the ache we felt. I listened to him and the nurse reviewing the past eight hours. It was as uneventful as we could have hoped for, but it was clear that Nora was not home free, either. Here, in contrast to prior hospital stays, the nurses were either in the room or watching from outside all night long. Literally everything, day or night, was done by the medical staff. Every beep and alarm was taken seriously—not a minute was lost in attending to them.

Tracey appeared a few minutes later, still stale from her night in the parents' quarters. We heard from Glenn that the first and second wave of medical entourages had already been through. We would learn throughout that day, and in those that followed, that Nora's case had attracted great interest. The stream of curious medical staff flowed all day.

Early that afternoon, we followed as Nora, her equipment and her entourage went to another floor to undergo a CAT scan of her brain. I surmised this wasn't a routine procedure, even for this surgery. It took an hour to prepare her for the move, readying all the attachments and transferring to transportable machines with meticulous care. We all followed her through the hallways, behind the rolling crib. Glenn went in with her. CAT scans are very sensitive at detecting recent bleeding and hemorrhages from trauma. I didn't know if they were concerned about yesterday's loss of blood, or if this had to do with the blood clot that no one else had seemed to hear mentioned. Subsequently, the report showed nothing significant or unusual.

Back in the ICU, Nora's epilepsy doctor stopped in. I thought her face somewhat belied her words… "She's doing well, I hear," she offered in her brogue, the sound of which still inexplicably washed a few shards of my emotional debris away. "… and no seizures? That's good news."

Of course that was good but, on the other hand, Nora was so sedated I wondered whether seizures could break through anyway. I didn't ask this question, because at the moment, getting Nora back was the important thing. Beyond that, I didn't care.

Except to get food or for sleep breaks, Tracey, Glenn and I hardly left the room. A sound or movement from Nora jerked us to attention and into motion if one of us was not already at her crib's side. I only felt a little better when I could sit near her and touch her. I wanted desperately for her to know we were there. When she moaned or stirred, we talked softly to her.

That night, I slept in the ICU with Nora. The bed, a window seat at the back of the room with a privacy curtain, made it more comfortable than the chair-beds we were used to. But, because this was intensive care, the nurse was in the room more often than not; moving around and tending to all the tubes, dripping medications, monitors and bags. Here, every single piece of equipment beeped and it was guaranteed that something would start just as I was about to fall asleep or when the nurse left the room. Unlike our other visits, there was nothing I could do for Nora except be there. The sleeping alcove was behind the head of her crib, and passage around to the front was largely constrained by equipment on either side. I could not see her from where I lay; if I heard her make any noise at all, I was on my feet, picking my way around the equipment to check on her.

The next morning was more awful, if that is possible. We'd been warned that the second-day post-op would be the worst in terms of swelling. They were right. It broke our hearts to look at her. Her legs and arms were so taut with fluid that they looked as if they might burst. Her face was distorted from swelling and her eyelids were so swollen that, even in the brief moments when she stirred and tried, she couldn't open them. All we could do was talk softly or sing her favorite songs, hoping she would know we were there. I would sit for long periods next to the crib with my hand on her. I needed her to know that she was not alone. At one point during that second day, when I touched her hand, she responded by wrapping her fingers around one of mine, letting me know she was there and knew I was, too. Otherwise, she moved very little, but it was a relief that when she did, she was able to move both her left and right sides.

At the 36-hour mark she was still highly sedated and her moments of consciousness were fortunately few. This was good for healing, but very scary for us. Her right eyelid now had such an intense shiner that the lid looked like it had a streak of blood just under the skin. She looked even worse than the day before, which was also alarming. She didn't resemble our Nora anymore and, because she was absent, it was as if the child we knew had all but disappeared. We all longed for her return.

On the foot of the crib facing the door, Tracey posted a pre-surgery photo of Nora. The photo clearly testified to the aura of light and the personality that was uniquely hers. It was important for us to show those who had not previously seen her, the real Nora: her luminous smile and vibrant blue eyes. The reminder only made me long for her all the more.

Together, the three of us danced to the lead of the medical staff. We moved about the hospital room doing nothing and everything we could to be our own salvation, while we waited with trepidation for the next bit of news, and ultimately for our Nora to reappear. The passing hours melted and draped themselves over us, like a live interpretation of Salvador Dali's painting "Persistence of Memory," with its melting clock faces. The painting's meaning is about the distortion of time in our dreams. For us, the dream was an extended nightmare.

As caretakers, Tracey, Glenn and I have very different personalities. Putting us all in one room with one focus is a feat in itself. I have the most empathetic bleeding heart. I ached with Nora's discomfort and couldn't bear seeing her experience pain. I could see that the medical staff was so intent upon their tasks they seemed at times to forget she was a five-month-old child.

Tracey is pragmatic. I don't mean to imply that she isn't emotional, but she always has her eye on the goal, seeking information to evaluate each step in pursuit of it. Glenn occupies an emotional position between ours, evaluating information differently; he feels deeply, but he's steady, not reactionary like I am.

I imagine they just put up with me at times, maybe more times than I even know. Often, comments were out of my mouth before I could contain them. This was something that amazed me. It really wasn't like me. At times it made us laugh and laughter was scarce.

One of those times was one of our first long-term monitoring visits. The nurse presented us with hospital-issue clothing for Nora. Without a second thought, I snatched it from her hand with a dismissal characteristic of royalty, saying, "Oh, no she's NOT wearing that!" In my own defense, this was because I couldn't bear the thought of that scratchy garment next to Nora's soft and delicate skin. Tracey was astounded at my imperious outburst.

"I couldn't believe you said that. You should have seen the look on the nurse's face," she told me later. We still laugh about it.

At the four-day mark, all of the tubes and wires were still attached. Each and every one hurt me. Of them all, the closest attention was always paid to the two drains expelling fluid from Nora's head. The amount and color of fluid was closely monitored and, without wanting to know the details, I could tell they were the most important indicators of additional bleeding and of pressure on her brain. It was not to be forgotten that the surgeon had not replaced the piece of bone in her head for that reason.

Pre-surgery, Tracey had been told that the breathing tube could probably be removed within the first 24 hours, but it still remained in place. It was a precaution; no time would be wasted if they had to rush Nora back into surgery. The fact that it was there told me that Nora was still in danger.

On January 19th, one of the drains was removed from Nora's head. This was a strong indicator that she was mending and her body's own powers of absorption were taking over. That was a milestone, and another one was that it was also my son's 40th birthday; we couldn't be with him to celebrate.

MORNINGS

Hospital mornings begin even earlier in the ICU than on the other floors. If you do get to sleep at all, you wake up even earlier. From the experience of my prior stays, I thought I knew the morning routine and even the cast of characters who visited. We saw many of the same faces here. However, in addition to them, the sheer number of people who visited Nora's room in the ICU during the morning rounds was overwhelming, indicating that Nora's surgery had much to teach. They came in no less than groups of four and often many times more. Sometimes it was difficult to fit them all into the room.

We must have been the first stop on rounds, because caravans began showing up as early as 5:00 a.m. There was no keeping track or trying to remember names when introduced, nor understanding who all these visitors were. I suppose in a teaching hospital, the most interesting cases are in the ICU. These observers asked a lot of questions: What kind of night did she have? Had she moved her right hand or leg? Were movements different or the same as before the surgery? Had we seen any seizures?

Sometimes they would ask permission to touch her and they commented among themselves and did a lot of staring. In all, I don't know if any of them had any idea what it felt like to be on our side of the crib. Few gave any indication that they did and I attribute that to their particular focus rather than to a lack of awareness or caring.

Because we were all really tired, living under such a microscope during such an emotional time was tough. Our lives were distorted and tentative. It was difficult to always be sharing this sacred space. We knew at these times, however, that someone had gone before us and that our trials were adding information for those who would follow.

It seemed, though, that everyone wanted a look at the baby girl who had somehow earned the title of "The Star of the ICU." Was that because this surgery was uncommon, or because Nora was one of the youngest to undergo it? Was it because Nora had prevailed over greater odds than we knew? We not so secretly felt that the "Star" title was likely a result of nothing more or less than wanting a dose of that Nora magic we knew so well—the magic of a miracle, of her pure desire to be here among us, regardless of the challenges or odds.

It may seem silly to mention this, but aside from everything else that was going on, it added to my personal discomfort that this particular ICU room has no bathroom. Under the circumstances, that might appear a frivolous complaint, but it did present a challenge. To get to the nearest restroom meant going outside the ICU to the public bathrooms just off the main hallway. Most often the barrage of morning rounds started before I could escape to pee or splash the remains of the night from my face. While, if I'd had one, I might have ducked into the room's bathroom for a minute; but without one, I wasn't leaving Nora in a room full of strangers, no matter who they were.

Sleeping in that room meant that I would often get caught still in bed, rising abruptly to stand vigil and entertain questions from the visitors. Most often, I'd get up as I heard the door open. Being without an adjoining bathroom put another kink in my bed-head. It meant I either had to be up before visitors struck, or be trapped until they left.

This is when I relinquished my last smidgeon of dignity. I remember well the first morning I scuffed out into the hallway. It was 8:30 a.m. by the time there was a break from our visitors. I was still in my sleeping clothes, braless, without my glasses or the benefit of a hairbrush. I hit the button to open the locked double doors that led to the public hallway. Shocked out of my intense focus on all things pertaining to Nora, I was jolted back into the real world, finding myself weaving my way through a bustling hallway full of people dressed in street clothes. I couldn't escape, so I played a childlike game of- *If I don't look at them, they can't see me*, to get through it, meanwhile experiencing what it might feel like to be a bag lady on Fifth Avenue.

Safely inside the restroom, mortification set in with one look in the mirror as I realized that the hardest part was yet to come; going back. Not only would I have to retrace my route, but this time I would be fully aware of how I looked. I'd have to get the attention of the receptionist and have her buzz me back in to the ICU.

I took a deep breath, left my vanity in the restroom and braved the hallway. No one cared, not even me.

Sent: Tuesday, January 20, 2009 11:10 AM
From: Tanya To: Wade
Subject: Today
Hi.
I sent you a photo of her. Did you get it? Nora was just lying there looking with both eyes open at Tracey. She's still very dazed, but we are beginning to see glimpses of the real Nora. She opens her eyes when she hears Tracey's voice.
She's still on a ton of medications. She's still swollen, but we see some improvement.
We still can't hold her. We all miss her so much.
I hope you are well. I am doing okay eating and such. I am tired.
I discovered that the Harvard Co-op bookstore is right across the street. I plan to go there later today. There's a book, The Power of Now that I have been wanting to read. Now seems like the time.
Seems like I have been gone forever; I miss you very much.

On the fifth day post-surgery, we finally began to see real progress. The medical staff removed Nora's two IVs, replacing one with a new one. They removed the catheter tube and she was back in diapers. One of the head drains was removed, which meant that she was off most of the monitoring. Finally, the horrible breathing tube that had been figuratively choking me, too, was removed. If the predictions of a ten-day post-op stay were correct, we still had one head drain, stitches, medications and at least five more days to go. This still felt arduous.

It was such a relief when Nora's breathing tube was removed and her entire face was finally unobstructed and the swelling was beginning to subside, taking with it the distortion. She was looking more like Nora. She was surfacing from sedation more frequently and opening her eyes. Although there was no real recognition in her face, it was clear she was hearing us. Best of all, we'd seen no seizures.

Tracey reintroduced Nora to her pacifier, hoping it might soothe her. She quickly and completely rejected it. We surmised that her throat was sore from the breathing tube, which had been inserted for so long that the motion of sucking exacerbated it. Her mouth and lips were dry and we used flavored swabs to moisten them, but she repeatedly pushed them out of her mouth with her tongue. We were told that this reaction could be the result of reflux; it could be thrush, a mild infection that would make it difficult or uncomfortable to swallow, or it could be a residual reaction to the breathing tube. We hoped it would subside, but ultimately it didn't.

It was sad and frustrating that we still couldn't offer Nora much comfort. It did seem, though, a stroke of good fortune that she had the G-tube. This meant that now, transitioning from the intravenous feedings, she could be fed via tube. Had we not had that option, she likely would have had to undergo the G-tube surgery before she could go home. At least we didn't have to put her through that.

The going was still slow in the transition to feeding. Her gag reflex was easily triggered, even if she wasn't taking fluids by mouth. She threw up, which was difficult and rather dangerous, for her head had to be restrained at a minimum angle to her body. The sound of her hoarse cry sounded pitiful; it tugged at my heart. Making up for it all, we weren't seeing any seizures.

Underlying all my worries about Nora, there was the nagging thought of the unfinished work I had hanging over my head. I was angry with myself for having promised to do it under these circumstances. I had let myself be pushed into it. At that point, I resented the client and berated myself. Exhausted and burned out, I still kept my word. That day, I sat with my laptop, numbly trying to make sense of the draft I had promised to write. Where I found the concentration, I don't know, but I finished as promised and delivered it on time.

Weeks later, after we'd returned home, the client approved the final copywriting and paid me for it, but as it turned out, they never produced the brochure. I'd compromised my own well-being when I should have just let it go and allowed the business world to get along without me.

Sent: Thursday, January 22, 2009, 2:00 PM
From: Tanya To: Wade
Subject: Day 6
Hi,
Tracey and I went to dinner last night at the restaurant across the street. The wine and the food tasted so good. To eat in a nice environment was great. I slept really well for the first time.
Nora has been vomiting. Too much tube feeding too fast I thought. They keep talking about getting her back to normal. I may have overstepped bounds, but I complained. How is any of this remotely

near normal? She's been lying there for days, we can't pick her up when she cries and she still won't take the pacifier for comfort. How can they expect her food consumption to be normal when nothing else is? Does the medical community still not realize we are whole beings?
Case in point, this morning, for the very first time since the surgery, Glenn got to hold her for about 90 minutes. Honestly, it made all the difference to her. You could see her relax. Her heart rate slowed … it was slower than any other time since we've been here.
They promised me that I can hold her later today. I can't wait.
We still are not sure when we are going to get out of ICU and go to the other floor. We're not anxious to leave. The attention and care are great.
We are all tired, but doing ok.
I miss you. I hope we are more than half the way there!

Nora and I turned a corner of well being when we got to hold her. When it was my turn, her eyes were bright and focused on my face, though it felt as if she were seeing through a haze. She looked straight up at me as I talked and sang to her. When she smiled at me, I could feel a part of myself coming back to life. The progress she made that day was noticeable. I was convinced that it was because we'd finally been able to hold her.

From that day on, we could almost see improvement every six hours and each little advance was encouraging. She was moving symmetrically and her strength was better than ever on her right side, which is something we expected, but it was a relief, too. Removing the final head drain was postponed several times. We knew we didn't want to be transferred out of the ICU before it was out, but we were anyway. Late in the evening of the seventh day, we moved to our old stomping grounds at 9 North. We were fortunate to get a private room there. In addition to waiting for the head drain and stitches to be removed, there were still unresolved matters, like the pesky business of reattaching the piece of skull bone that sat frozen somewhere, waiting. And most of all, we waited to find out if she would need to go back in the future for another surgery to finish what was started, or was this enough? We'd have to wait and see.

By the eighth day post-op, Nora was awake more than she was asleep and was unbelievably full of energy and smiles, though she did get cranky easily. The last drain was finally removed on the morning of the ninth day and the bandages were all removed.

Glenn left just after that to return to Connecticut, and shortly after, the physical therapist showed up to get Nora moving. Nora complained and it gave me a headache to see her head being moved about.

The incision was still stitched, but it all looked good. I am typically squeamish, but I found that I wasn't totally repelled by the sight of it. The left side of her little head was, of course, shaved, and because the bone was missing, it protruded more than the other side. The surgical stitches ran on the side of her head, from just in front of her ear upward in a curved line to the crest of her head and then back down, ending at a point midway between the back of her head and her ear. The stitched shape reminded me and others of the curved stitched seams on the cover of a softball. I was just happy to have her back and to be able to hold her without the damned drain coming out of the top of her head.

The stitches were removed on day ten. During this process, I put in a rather embarrassing and loud vocal performance of "Nora tunes" directed at distracting her. Unfortunately, it also had to be endured by the entire staff in attendance, and Tracey, if not Nora herself. I guess it made me feel better. Knowing Tracey, it probably drove her crazy, but she let me go on, racking up another funny moment among the painful ones.

The surgeon decided that Nora would be going home without the bone he'd removed from her head. She would have to return later for surgery to reattach it. We'd done all right handling her in the hospital with a large soft spot above her right ear, but the thought of taking her home in this condition was scary. At the last minute, we were sent down to the prosthetics lab to have her fitted for a protective helmet. The technician twisted and turned Nora's head and neck in odd ways, to take the measurements. That, and the fact that it was feeding time, caused her to cry. Due to the tube-feeding process, we were without the ability to satisfy her and since the surgery the pacifier was no longer a solution, either.

We were almost to the finish line, and I'd used up all my strength and endurance. I just wanted to haul off and hit someone, but I made it through and Nora did, too…not one seizure.

Sent: Monday, January 26, 11:50 PM
From: Tanya To: Wade
Subject: Maybe tomorrow
It's almost midnight and I am hanging out here with Miss Nora waiting for her next feeding. She's doing well. I think you will be amazed at how her personality is re-emerging. She's quite smiley and spunky for sure.

I will be glad to get home, and yet coming away from this intense focus, I really don't know how to put life back together. I really just don't know. This experience has had an undeniable effect on me, but I can't say yet what it is or how it will manifest itself.
It looks like we can go home tomorrow. I can't wait to see you!

I'd completely forgotten until much later that January 26th was also Tracey and Glenn's third wedding anniversary.

Late the next day, we were discharged. As we prepared for our journey home, I stayed in the hospital room and tended to Nora and her farewell-to-Boston feeding, while Tracey took the car back to the hospital housing to pack and load up all our belongings. While I waited, I sat alone in the hospital room in the pure luxury of rocking Nora in my arms after she'd dropped off to sleep; no tubes, wires, or other connections. I was enveloped in peace. I sat for almost 30 uninterrupted minutes of intense, joyous awareness of how lucky we were to be where we were at that minute and for the evidence of miracles in my life.

The door opened and in walked Tracey. "I need to thank you," I said. "I want to thank you for the gift of this incredible child."

She looked understandably puzzled.

FLUTTERS

Never before had the privacy of home and our own soft, dark and quiet beds felt so delicious. It took Nora much less time to adjust to being back home than it did the rest of us. We inched back into our routines at a snail's pace. Despite the crazy half-bald haircut, the bulge in her head where the bone was supposed to be, and the killer scar, Nora's bright smile and typical-for-her behavior gave little indication of the ordeal she'd been through. Seeing no seizures was delightful. We sometimes had to remind ourselves of the horror of them to truly appreciate their absence, even though she would continue on anti-seizure medications for at least another year.

Nora quickly returned to her dates with the physical therapists. I joined as many as I could, learning how her therapists were working with her under post-surgical constraints. At nearly six months old, seizures, medications and her low muscle tone had delayed Nora's physical development significantly. Unlike typical children at her age, she could not sit on her own without being propped up on all sides. She was unable to roll over. When I look back at videos of this phase, I can see how medicated she was and find it hard to imagine how she made any progress at all.

On one of the first few days of February, I was at Tracey's house waiting for Tina, the therapist, to arrive. Nora was sitting in her carrier seat on the kitchen counter and I was standing in front of her, playing and talking to her. Her eyelids fluttered for just a few seconds. *A seizure?* Fear-induced electric shock ran through me. *No!* My breath caught in my throat and I remained speechless as Tracey entered the room, but I couldn't disguise the distress on my face. "What is it?" she asked.

"I think I just saw her eyes flutter."

"I know," she said. "We've seen a few. They said we might ... that it's not uncommon after surgery ... hopefully healing. You know."

Over the next few days these eye flutters continued at a rate of several a day. It wasn't clear exactly what they were. Nora was due back for a follow-up visit in Boston the second week of February. By the time Tracey and Glenn took her back, it seemed clearer that what we were seeing were mild seizures.

On that visit to Boston, an EEG showed that it was minor seizure activity, originating from the same side of the brain as before; likely the site where the surgery had not been completed. Both the neurologist and the neurosurgeon thought that another surgery, to complete the final 25% of the hemispherectomy, was necessary. At that time, they would also replace the piece of bone in Nora's head, which was still "on ice," and could remain stored under refrigeration for almost a year.

No date was set for the second surgery. The surgeon really wanted to give Nora time to grow, waiting anywhere from three to 18 months. The neurologist, on the other hand, wanted to see surgery done as soon as possible, in the hopes that Nora would then be seizure-free. Once again, the path for the immediate future was to try to control the seizures with medication.

Also during that checkup in Boston, Nora had the final fitting for her helmet. We'd been handling her since surgery, being excruciatingly careful of the huge soft spot on the side of her head. They brought her helmet home, but she never wore it.

Nora's next visit to Boston was scheduled in three months, but it happened sooner. She had been vomiting on and off since surgery and, in the last few days of February, it became more frequent. We knew that vomiting after brain surgery could indicate fluid or pressure on the brain. A call to the pediatrician and a call to the neurologist confirmed that Nora needed to return to Boston for a CAT scan immediately, to assess the situation.

We were duly scared.

Tracey, Nora and I left the next day at five a.m. to be in Boston for her eight a.m. appointment; the scan was scheduled for late morning. Nora needed to be asleep for the test. The hospital staff was well versed in making us comfortable and being patient, in waiting for Nora to fall asleep. We were given a room with a cot and a rocking chair. If Nora would go to sleep on her own, they could conduct the test without having to anesthetize her. They told us not to worry, that we had as long as it would take to get her to sleep. If and when she was, we could call them and it would take only a few minutes to get her in for the test. The test itself would take about ten minutes in total. Both Tracey and I knew we'd have to relax so Nora would.

Forty minutes later we were ushered down the hall, sleeping Nora in arms, to a large, dimly lit, high-ceilinged room. Approximately 12 feet away, in front of us to our right, was the machine. It looked like a huge donut with a 10-foot long table extending out from the hole. I'd seen one only on television. This was much more frightening. The donut was decorated with a collage of kid-friendly stickers, which had the opposite effect on me. Like a scary clown, it gave me the chills which were aided by the extremely cool temperature of the room. In the dim light, the back wall of the room was decorated with an outer-space-themed mural that stretched up to meet the unusually high ceiling.

The nurse instructed Tracey to place Nora on the table, close to the donut. Together they bundled her against the cold, while another aide helped me into the required leaded x-ray-proof jacket, donned backward to protect my chest. Tracey joined me, slipping on hers. To our left was the glassed-in booth where the technician was readying the machine. We waited, having much too much time to look across the room, at tiny Nora who looked even tinier against the length of the table, her little body taking up a mere fraction of it. She was wrapped in white. Her body and her head were strapped down. I felt as though we were living out a scene from a weird science fiction movie, offering Nora up to some kind of crazy experiment.

The machine started to buzz and I held fast to my hope that she would remain asleep. She did.

From where I stood, behind and to the left of Tracey, I watched my daughter as she watched the moving table slide her baby into the hole of the donut, aware that rays were probing the depths of her brain matter; another ugly, yet awesome, medical miracle. I couldn't escape into my head; something in me demanded I stay present. I trembled as I thought, here we are again, experiencing something impossible to grasp as part of our lives.

As soon as it was over, I let it all go. With Nora back in Tracey's arms, we were whole again for the moment and it felt so good.

The test revealed that there were no bad surprises and nothing to worry about. Nora likely had a normal flu bug. Something that is so ordinary for other typically healthy children had sent us on a trip to another planet.

ROAD MAPS

"I am on the road, but still in northern Massachusetts," says my daughter, her voice garbled across the cellular connection. "She's sleeping right now...kinda rough night, didn't want to go to sleep...woke up a few times. She threw up a few times yesterday...I think dealing with post-nasal stuff. But she's happy, smiling, I dunno," her voice trails a bit just as the slip-knot that's taken up residence in my stomach tightens.

I can picture the pink, rear-facing car seat that holds the object of my affection. I don't picture the scar, but I feel it in my heart. I've been pining all weekend for them. They've traveled out of state for a visit with Tracey's former college roommate and are on their way back. As we talk, I want to reach across miles to scoop them up and pluck them from their journey, to keep them safe so my heart can be safe too from the million dangers that I worry are always lurking, as if I could ever save them from life. Of course I can't, but I always feel I can take better care of them than anyone else. What is this emotion I feel? Is it control? The intensity of my feeling tells me it obviously needs examining and editing before I dare express it. It's familiar and yet seems dangerous, like clinging too hard when you should let go. I realize that taking care of them is really taking care of me, not that they don't benefit in some way. There's conflict within me.

I have become a student of my daughter's voice, learning to listen for an uncharacteristic pause, a sigh or sharp breath, a particular tone, a warble in the steadiness. I attempt to ascertain her level of stress or concern. I wonder if she has any idea that I do that. Will her daughter be as unknown to her as she often is to me? We are very different. I have no idea what it feels like for her to be on the other end of a conversation with me. What bothers me most is that I have no idea what it is like to be an adult daughter talking with her mother.

I tread carefully, avoiding anything I can think of that might annoy Tracey. I am never sure that I succeed. Is this normal, or what is normal? For sure, it is complicated. I have a suspicion that this wariness is a generational thing. And I am beginning to wonder if that's part of what makes being a grandparent magical. Again, I have little experience being a granddaughter, either.

My mother's mother was a small woman who always looked older than her age. Her life must have been hard, because even in early photos of her when my mother was young, my grandmother looked old; her thin face was carved with wrinkles.

For as long as I could remember, she'd lived with my aunt. My grandmother only spoke Hungarian. I remember seeing her sitting on the sofa in my aunt's house while we visited. She was rather scary and certainly not grandmotherly. She was most often speechless, except when she would yell at us in Hungarian. I never knew what she was shouting about. She and I never enjoyed even one intelligible interaction. I don't even know if she knew who I was. That she was the one who appeared in my vision on the way to the hospital for Nora's birth still seems strange to me. Perhaps it was a message in itself, a message I have yet to understand. She died several years after my mother did.

My father's mother died when I was about four years old. I can picture only one memory of her: She is ill. Bedridden. She is staying at our house. She's in my parents' bed. I am sitting on the floor near the bed. We aren't talking; I just sit there because it feels good. My mother comes into the room with a tray, on it is a cup of tea and a plate of cinnamon toast (a staple in our lives). My mother places the tray beside my grandmother and then leaves the room.

My grandmother breaks a piece of toast and offers it to me. I take it because I want it, not just to be polite, as I am otherwise likely to do. It tastes better than my favorite birthday cake and I feel how delighted my grandmother is to have me there, sharing it with her. My mother returns and scolds me for eating food meant for my grandmother. My grandmother comes to my rescue. She died not long after that.

I've never thought much about that or about my grandmothers until I became one myself. I have no role model for mothering or grandmothering, but then I also feel no pressure of having to live up to any. In that, I am both free and lost.

ANOTHER LOOK

Early in March, Nora's seizures continued to be minimal—very slight eye flutters and occasional shoulder jerks. Except for her delayed physical development, one would hardly notice anything unusual about her.

Tracey, Nora and I made the day trip back to Boston for Nora's first post-surgery visit with the surgeon. Though she had been back since the surgery, she had not actually been to see him. This would be my first time in his office.

When we entered, he was at his desk completing some paperwork. He asked us to give him a few minutes to finish up dictating notes into a recorder.

Tracey, Nora and I sat waiting on a bench against the wall. His desk was across the room at a 90-degree angle to us and, though he acknowledged us, he hadn't yet turned his head to actually look at us.

Looking around the room, I saw his family photo. It seemed odd that he has had such a profound impact on our family and we knew nothing about his. The only other revealing thing in the office was on the wall, a framed article featuring him in *Fast Company* magazine.

I would describe him as a pleasant, energetic man with a straightforward surgical approach to everything I'd seen him do when Nora was in ICU post-surgery. It made me wonder if, when he looked at Nora, he saw her as an individual, or just her brain.

While we sat waiting, I was also waiting to watch his reaction when he finally looked at Nora. Being elated by how wonderfully she was doing, I was curious to know what he thought. I had paid close attention to every doctor's reaction to Nora, always looking for something some clue to what each was thinking about her. Doctors seem to know how to be careful with words, but body language and facial expressions often expose what they won't say, be it bad or good. I always looked for those clues, as on the day of Nora's surgery.

Finally, he turned toward us and scooted on his rolling desk chair over to where we sat…me next to Tracey, who was holding Nora. Because all four of us were seated, he was already at eye-level with us all, but his eyes stayed focused on the floor as he traveled across the room. He didn't raise them to the level of ours until he was seated directly in front of Nora. Only then did he raise his eyes, to look directly into her face. He placed his hand on either side of her face, pausing with the intensity of a coin collector examining a rare coin, he finally spoke, "You are a sight for sore eyes," he said.

I felt certain that what he and Nora had experienced that day in January was significant for both of them, in ways we would never know. I still believe there was something more to know and her recovery may have been more tenuous than we were aware of, but now it made no difference, except to be grateful for the moment, and how fortunate we were.

SPRING

Life goes on. Sure, it does. Tell that to anyone who has experienced Post Traumatic Stress Disorder. To describe our situation that way might sound dramatic, but there is evidence to support it. Regardless of how things might have looked externally, I felt emotionally wounded. I felt as if I'd had come close to drowning and was so exhausted I could barely tread water. I needed time to surface, to breathe, but it wasn't all over: We had to face a second surgery.

I needed time to absorb this and was not in the mood to be with happy people. Tracey reacted differently, at least from what I could see. She was doing all she could to find and create some normalcy in her life, while I just wanted to hide. Although I never asked, "Why my child? "Why my grandchild?" I was angry. I'd learned very early that life wasn't fair; should I have been surprised? Still, I felt I needed time and sought refuge from the rest of the world.

When I encountered people who knew me, they were generally considerate in asking about Tracey and Nora. Listening was another matter. I believe that listening has become a lost art anyway. I think that this new world of social media, what I call "living life out loud", represents the individual's cry to be heard. We all need that. At this time, I needed that, too, when at other times I would have been the listener.

I find that many people I meet don't know how to listen or have a real conversation anymore. They simply want to talk about themselves and most do, almost endlessly, if you let them.

For my work, I interview people often and to do what I do, I must listen carefully. I am truly interested in what they have to say. In social interactions, I am often the first one to ask a question, which makes me a soft touch for people who love to talk endlessly about themselves, as many do. Some do ask questions, which most often are thinly disguised vehicles to enable them to tell you what they think. I know this, and as such I can only think that my state of mind at this time must have caused me to lose perspective. I began to realize that I had to relinquish my expectations and my anger. I needed to acknowledge to myself that I was in a very fragile state and needed to avoid social situations. It was new for me to protect myself and risk others' opinions of me.

Though I hibernated from time to time, there was still happiness in the world around me. It was good to know it was there even though I wasn't sure that outside of Nora's smile I would feel it again. I could dismiss the rest of the world, but family was the inner circle. I still had to face two social events: one was Nora's christening, the other was my son's upcoming May wedding.

Early in the spring, Tracey and Glenn planned to re-baptize Nora at their church. I am not religious, but I respect the beliefs and rituals others choose to follow. Tracey and Glenn had leaned on and been supported throughout by their faith. I was grateful that it helped them endure and I thought it was great that they would have an event to celebrate.

In the chaos surrounding Nora's entry into the world, all the usual celebrations had fallen by the wayside. Parents of special needs children, and the people who love them, miss out on that. Time gets stolen by worry; people outside the circle feel awkward and don't know what to do. The family naturally longs for as many moments of normalcy as possible. They want and deserve to celebrate their child. That need does not vanish—in fact, it may be even stronger. I don't think that those outside the circle realize this.

The christening was not to be a big, elaborate event as some are; just the church ritual and a reception with cake and coffee in the church hall afterward. Almost everyone who was invited attended. I knew the count of the RSVPs and yet when the day arrived, I was overwhelmed. The lack of hoopla made it even clearer to me that most people came not for a party, but to celebrate Nora. This christening was one way that they all could come together in support of Nora and her family. So many of them were delighted to finally meet the Nora they had heard so much about. People shared with me how they had forgone other plans to be part of the celebration and how they had followed and shared Nora's journey and her progress with others who did not even know our family. Seeing everyone and the feeling of their support flowed through me with warmth and comfort. For the first time, I saw the benefit of going to church and having the support of a community. This was something my religious experience had never included. I discovered the power, healing and joy that can come from community.

PERFECT STORM

Woven into the new fabric of life that spring were plans for my son's May wedding. I've read that the role of mother of the groom can sometimes feel like being a key player in a game in which you don't know the rules. It's all about the bride yet, as the mother of the groom, this is still your child getting married. It's a delicate position, requiring that ego be left behind. That's not a complaint, it is just what I have heard from others who have gone before me. My state of distraction was still intense and I felt disconnected anyway.

Maggie, the bride, had immediate family spread all over the country, leaving some of the usual pre-wedding social events, like a bridal shower, forgone at her request. I realized then how such events help to acquaint and foster connections between both families before the wedding. The wedding was to be a destination event for everyone, in Cape Cod. I visited the venue with my son and his bride-to-be for one of the planning trips. It was a lovely, elegant, water view setting and the plans sounded grand.

From the outside looking in, weddings are exciting, joyous and fun events. Viewed from the inside, they are as complicated as it gets, in terms of making your own dreams come true, while attempting to keep everyone else happy. My experience is that they are stressful beyond belief. There is nothing more crazy-making than family opinions, decisions on who to include, who to exclude, who should pay and who is responsible for what. Are traditional roles being followed? What's the etiquette, and does anyone care? Then there is the blending of two families. Regardless of the push and pull of planning, when the day comes it all usually works out just fine.

Your child's wedding is an emotional event, another one of those that is full of expectation about how things should be. The expectations can be overwhelming. For me, the month of May was shaping up to be landmark, like one of those perfect storms that brews long and from afar and then all forces converge at the same time and place.

I had been working for the previous eighteen months writing the script for an eight-part video project for a large hospital. As luck would have it, the two-day video shoot was scheduled for the Monday and Tuesday after the wedding. How these things happen I still wonder.

It was a tricky project and getting final script approval had been difficult, but finally it was approved, and while the time for the client's approval process can lag, once they "pull the trigger", no waiting is acceptable. I was needed onsite during the shoot for last-minute edits. Some post-wedding recovery time would have been lovely. This was a landmark project for me, so I didn't want to miss the videotaping.

Spring was also an intense time for Tracey's job. She needed more time to work, so I scheduled my time to help fill in and be with Nora, including helping out with keeping her therapy appointments. The week before the wedding, we were all busy with the usual last-minute preparations, including packing for the trip to the Cape. Nora had her usual calendar full of medical and therapy appointments.

As the date neared, we were all looking forward to the wedding, to getting away and being near the ocean. It was such a wonderful opportunity to let go a little, get dressed up instead of living in sweats, see family and friends and celebrate together. Tracey would be standing up with her brother, taking the role of best "man", while Maggie's brothers were acting "bridesmaids".

Tracey and I had shopped for dresses and shoes and only my choice of earrings remained. I shopped everywhere for these but, for some reason, nothing made me happy. Other than this small detail, we were all ready to go.

During the months just prior, Tracey had had some bouts of severe indigestion, like the one she experienced during our hospital stay the previous December. Given the stress of her work schedule and all of Nora's needs and appointments, it wasn't surprising. Stress engenders illness. I should have been more concerned.

On Wednesday, three days before the wedding, Tracey suffered another bout of severe indigestion. This time the pain was worse than ever. I took her to the doctor, with Nora in tow. He found nothing amiss, but sent her for blood work. The three of us went to the lab, this time for Tracey, and then I took them home.

That evening the pain became too severe to ignore, sending her to the emergency room. Though the symptoms had not been characteristic, the ER tests indicated a gallbladder problem. Tracey was admitted that evening. Nora was with me.

In addition to the pain she was in, she was frantic about the wedding. While it was likely she would need to have her gallbladder removed at some point, her doctor said he could provide relief for her by performing a laparoscopic procedure to remove the gallstones that were causing the pain. He said it was a simple procedure and promised she would still make the wedding on Saturday.

I couldn't shake the weird coincidence that Tracey was exactly the same age as my mother was at the time she died from gall bladder surgery.

Tracey underwent the laparoscopic procedure early on Thursday morning but, instead of bringing relief, the pain was worse. She ended up having a case of pancreatitis, a very painful condition which was actually caused by the procedure. She was in pain, on medication, upset, but still determined to make it to Cape Cod by Friday for the rehearsal. Only time would tell.

Because Nora was staying with me, I couldn't visit Tracey in the hospital, which was frustrating. The pressure was on because, regardless of what was happening with Tracey, Wade and I had to be at the Cape for the church rehearsal by 4 o'clock on Friday. The rehearsal dinner, hosted by us, would follow. We turned Nora over to Glenn on Friday morning. I was sick at having to leave them behind, but I had no choice.

Within the first twenty miles of the trip, our car's check-engine light came on. There was no time to stop. It stayed on for the entire five-hour journey, which felt much longer. Instead of being excited, my heart was heavy at leaving Tracey behind and in the hospital, to boot. I could never have imagined that I would leave town while my daughter was in the hospital, yet here I was on the road. Hadn't we all been through enough? Didn't we deserve a break? Instead of happily anticipating the fun, the familiar lead weight was riding in my stomach again. I was angry. Tracey had been looking forward to enjoying the change of scene and the celebration, and I feared for how her illness would impact my son on his big day. At that moment, it was all in limbo. Where was I going to find the emotional reserve to rise to the occasion, and transform myself into the celebratory mother of the groom by the time I reached the Cape? I had no idea.

We arrived at the hotel barely in time for the rehearsal. I mustered my resolve to get into the swing of things. Without time to change clothes or freshen up, photos of the church rehearsal show a faded, rumpled woman looking dazed. I was.

My ex-husband, the kids' father, stood in for Tracey, taking her role for the rehearsal. As she had requested, I took photos and tried to remember the details so I could recount them to her on the day of the wedding. It all should have been such fun, but instead I felt like I was being split in two. Worry about both of my children caused my emotions to bounce between the two of them.

Back at the hotel, with only time for a quick wardrobe change, we were off to the rehearsal dinner. As it turned out, it was fortunate that we had been relieved of the actual planning of the dinner, since it was Maggie and her mom's wish to handle it. We also felt fortunate, because Wade and I could never have pulled off all those inevitable last-minute details under the circumstances. Thanks to the love of my family and more than a few glasses of wine, I found my center and made it. I won't say I wasn't conflicted; I was. As much as I was sad and I mourned the way the night should have been, what was worse was that I actually felt guilty because I somehow felt that I was being disloyal, allowing myself to have fun under the circumstances.

That feeling was further challenged during the evening when my son pulled us aside to say that the following Monday he was going to Manhattan to audition for a small part in a major movie. How exciting! But I felt the insanity of one child achieving extreme highs while the other had been down and was hitting bottom again. What an emotional tug of war, and what a test.

Saturday, the day of the wedding, Tracey called. We were both in tears as she told me she would not be coming. She was not feeling any better. Glenn and the girls were very disappointed as well. Each person impacted by this phone call had his or her own perspective. Maggie and her mom had to scurry through last-minute seating changes and altering place cards and seating charts because the absence of Tracey and family meant that their table would now have only two people at it. My son was without a best man; his father would now take Tracey's place, which also meant reading Tracey's toast.

This was not the way it was supposed to be. It was clear that I had to make a choice; to be in the moment or wallow in how I wished things could have been. With little time to adjust, I practiced what I had learned from my lessons with Nora. I knew that focusing on the present moment was the only real answer. I'd like to say I accomplished this gracefully, but rather think that martinis carried me a good deal of the way.

Tracey had given me the perfect pair of earrings to wear that day. When I put them on, and as I touched them throughout the evening, I allowed myself to miss her and honor my sadness.

On the way home, the car's check-engine light came on again and remained on all the way. When we reached home, I went straight to the hospital to see Tracey. She was doing better, though not yet recovered. She was scheduled to be released on Wednesday.

I brought her the centerpiece flowers from my table and the favors, but talking about the wedding hurt, making me feel uncomfortable. I knew how sad she was about missing it and felt I was making her even sadder.

When Monday arrived, Glenn needed to leave Nora with me, so I had no choice but to miss the video shoot. Nora had a doctor's appointment, her nine-month checkup at the pediatrician's. It felt wrong that Tracey wasn't there, especially because this was a "well-baby" visit for a change. The doctor was in disbelief when I told her about our wedding weekend and that Tracey was still in the hospital. "How did you handle it?" she asked.

"I learned that the only way to do it is one minute at a time. You can usually get through anything if you take it one minute at a time. I learned that from this one," I said, gesturing toward Nora, who was sitting half-naked on my lap.

At that moment, my cell phone text-message alert beeped. I would not have bothered with it under the circumstances, but I thought it might be Tracey calling about something relevant to the appointment. Instead, it was an excited message from my son, who was elated about being in Manhattan and waiting for his audition. I simply couldn't switch gears. My hands were full of Nora and my head of medical details; I couldn't respond.

Why do these things keep happening at exactly the same moment? Suddenly, I was oddly reminded of a scene in the movie *Evan Almighty*. When "God"

(Morgan Freeman), says to Evan (Steve Carell) regarding Evan's concerns about the challenge of building an ark, having no tools or skills, "When people ask me for courage, do you think I give them courage? No, I give them the opportunity to act courageously." I decided that with all that had happened in the past week, I was being challenged by something I needed to learn.

The next day, exhausted, I went to my client's video shoot. It was a long and exciting day. Ultimately, it turned out that, after all, the hospital never completed funding the project, so the video was never used.

The car's check-engine light never came back on.

TESTS

The summer of 2009 remained pretty much a blur. Nora's seizures continued to be mild. She was responsive and delightful to be around; a truly happy baby. We were grateful, but was this really Nora, or was it medication that made her so? There was no way to tell.

There were times when I couldn't ignore my feelings as I pushed the second and sometimes third syringe of meds into her feeding tube. Sometimes my aversion to pumping chemicals into her would make me gag. They didn't stop the seizures; really we had no idea if they were even effective, or what side-effects they might be having. We had never known Nora without them.

Though there was the threatening cloud of another surgery always hanging over us, we certainly were not sitting idly by, waiting for her to grow. Tracey was adamant about keeping up with plans, people and schedules for the variety of therapies that focused on Nora's continued health and developmental progress. That meant that Nora had at least one and sometimes two therapy appointments every day. Added to that schedule was an array of appointments with specialists.

We knew that Nora's seizures, and maybe even her medications, contributed to the delay in her development, but we didn't know what we could expect from her. It was clear that the diminished capabilities of her right arm and leg were related to the damaged part of her brain that controlled them. All of a sudden, the words cerebral palsy had meaning for me. It's the brain's connections, their malfunction, damage or loss that was the cause. The amazing wonder of our nature is that our brains are malleable or changeable. In Nora's case, therapy could help her to map the functionality she'd lost to a different part of her brain. The wisdom of her body had recognized the problem, and her miracle, which was unrealized at the time of my first video of her in the nursery, was that she was moving both arms and legs…her brain had started remapping before she was even born. But, whether it was due to her brain, brain surgery, or medication, at nine months old she was still unable to roll over or sit up without support. Her physical therapists were working with her, and teaching us how to facilitate the movements that would strengthen her muscles and provide the sensory input necessary to create the new brain connections.

In addition to these issues, the prolonged time she had been kept on the breathing tube after surgery had caused her to have an oral aversion; except for her fingers, Nora rejected anything else in her mouth. Oral therapy sessions, which were based on a process of desensitization to overcome the oral aversion, were the most difficult of the therapies for me to participate in. Early sessions involved the therapist sticking her finger inside Nora's mouth in order to stimulate and massage it. I knew it also served to strengthen muscles, and sensitize the tissue as well as desensitize her aversion, but it was forcefully invasive and Nora hated it.

Nora's doctors offered little speculation or reassurance about what we could expect her to achieve. Her therapists were more encouraging, always commenting that, based on Nora's energetic spirit, if anything was possible, she would succeed. One undeniable trait was that, despite it all, she was always eager to engage with everyone, loved attention, and rewarded us with smiles and babbles of communication.

In mid-July, the three of us, Tracey, Nora and I, packed up the car again for a five-day trip to Boston for another MRI and several days of extended EEG monitoring. By now, we were well practiced at travel, but on this trip, we left for the hospital later than usual in the evening. Nora was cranky; she squirmed in my arms at the rest stop.. I was holding her while the machine pumped her final feed for the night into her. I was frustrated, tired and hungry; my coping skills were red-lining. Tracey was in better shape than me, which wasn't saying much. Our own needs always took a backseat, simply because there was always so much to manage at home before embarking on these trips. Nora and I were cranky and I knew I was just not up to making the rest of the trip. We spent the night at a hotel near the rest stop.

The next morning, once again Tracey, Nora and I waited in a small holding room in the radiology department, Tracey sitting Indian-style on the cot against the wall, happy Nora splayed and spilling over her legs. I rocked in the rocking chair.

The nurse had already given Nora the injection of sedative that would put her to sleep. She'd be back in twenty minutes; enough time for the sedative to take hold.

It was happening again…that awful process that turns the otherwise-magical, sweet sight of a sleeping baby into something chilling. Tracey cuddled Nora more closely and we both focused on her little face. The room was quiet for a hospital, which is weird in itself. We didn't talk; we just both watched Nora's face for signs of sleep. In a few minutes, she began to doze. I looked up through a salty blur to see my own sadness reflected in my daughter's face.

When the nurse returned to take Nora away for the test, Tracey and I both fell to the side without purpose, like two bookends left askew on the shelf when the books are taken away. With that, we did what we could do. We went to the waiting room, pretending that we were sure everything would turn out alright and that we didn't hate every minute of it.

After an eternity, someone came to get us. In recovery, Nora was deathly still. I just wanted her to wake up and smile, but we were told she would likely be asleep for another fifteen minutes. A half hour passed. Anxiety had its grip on me and my mind raced with headlines of stories that told of anesthesia gone wrong. I have never trusted it. Each and every time it was as if we had never been through this before. The child in the next bed, who'd arrived in recovery after Nora, had already awakened.

Another fifteen minutes passed. I wanted to explode. Finally, we began to see signs. She was stirring, groggy and complaining, no smile; no matter, we had her back.

Once again, we made it through and moved on. Nora was admitted for the monitoring; the leads (wired connections) were glued to her scalp and her head once again was wrapped in a white turban. How, despite this, she was able to look angelic was beyond me.

We settled into the long-term monitoring routine. We expected to be here for several days. I would sleep in the hospital; Tracey would stay in the offsite housing. The monitoring was to confirm exactly how many seizures Nora was really having, because, as before, we only knew what we could see. More importantly, we hoped it would confirm that the seizures were emanating from the portion of Nora's brain that remained connected. This was vitally important. If it was, it meant that completing this surgery could end the seizures once and for all.

Fortunately, Nora and her brain were so obliging that the monitoring captured all it needed in the first twenty-four hours, in contrast to the three days we'd planned for. We wouldn't leave until the monitoring results were reviewed, should they need something more from her. Except for our concern over the results, the time we spent was comparatively easy for us all. Nora was comfortable, not in any distress, which relieved our stress as well. As it turned out, the report we received about the results of the test were not what we expected.

Mid-morning on the following day, fortunately both Tracey and I were in the hospital room with Nora. I say fortunately, because that is not always the case at that time of day and also, because, had either of us been there alone, the other would not have believed what happened.

I was standing on the window-side of the crib, Tracey on the other side of it with her back to the door. An epilepsy doctor, whom we did not normally see, came bursting into the room, followed by two other white-coated men. The doctor was clearly excited, an excitement that radiated from the others who trailed him. They were barely into the room when the doctor threw up his hands in exclamation. "It's good news!" he declared. "She's not having any seizure activity at all." He was clearly delighted.

Tracey and I were startled by this odd declaration and we froze in place. Sharing the impulse of disbelief, our eyes met and we telepathically flashed each other the same unspoken question: *What the heck is he talking about?* Her face mirrored the astonishment I felt. We both knew the other was thinking the same thing: *This is nuts! How do we tell him he's crazy without offending him?*

We held back our laughter and for fear of being rude, though we both recognized the urge in each other's eyes... a rare occurrence in this place. So rare in fact, that I had already gone beyond the situation in my head, seeing us all as though we were part of a scene in a sitcom, knowing full well that I would replay this scene in years to come.

We stood there speechless, seeing the puzzled look on the doctor's face, as he clearly wondered why we were not jumping for joy. We both struggled, our minds engaged in a game of mental jousting as we each attempted to form words appropriate for the situation ... no rulebook for this one.

Tracey looked at me and saw that I was waiting for her to do the talking. "Hmmm, we see her having seizures all the time. Why, just a few minutes ago. . ."

His face fell in confusion. Retracing his steps artfully, he offered an explanation. We eventually came to understand from him, and later from other doctors, why he would have reached such a conclusion.

Ultimately, the actual report told us that what we'd hoped was true: "electricity" was coming from the portion of her brain that was still connected. Completing the surgery that was aborted was still a hope for ending the seizures. Nora was scheduled to return for the surgery in three months, on October 28th.

All the medical indicators pointed to this being an easier surgery for Nora and for her surgeon. By the date of this surgery, Nora would be fifteen months old. Her age and increased size alone should mitigate some of the original risks. The remaining resection or disconnection would be much smaller in scope than the first surgery. And this time there would be no skull bone to cut through. It had been kept on ice, waiting to be reunited with her, and reattaching it would be part of the completion of the surgery. We knew that surgery wouldn't be any easier on us; it could even prove more difficult. Some of the anxiety we felt was from wondering what would happen if it didn't end the seizures, but this was not the time to pursue that train of thought further.

As we ignored counting the days until the surgery, Nora turned one year old in August. Tracey planned a big birthday party for her at home, complete with musical entertainment. The day of the party, I attended alone, because Wade was out of state. I sat with Nora on the blanket in the yard, as she watched the entertainer Tracey had hired for the children. Nora was mesmerized by his singing and guitar-playing. Her stunning blue eyes shone and sparked with interest, becoming as round with wonder as the huge blue polka dots on her party dress. I was so grateful to be holding her, sharing the experience. I wondered why and how Tracey allowed me to have these particular moments. It felt selfish to take them, but I ignored it and enjoyed each moment for the gift I knew it was.

There were at least 25 guests in attendance and, though I knew them all, I couldn't socialize as I normally would have. I was distracted, finding it difficult to be interested in anything or anyone. That in itself distressed me. I thought it was so wonderful that Tracey could plan and enjoy the party with all she had to contend with, and despite the surgery that still loomed, she created an air of normalcy. I was set off kilter by all the people around and the party had the opposite effect on me. To me, they all felt like intruders and it made me realize how intensely, and maybe dangerously connected I was to the two of them, having spent so many cloistered days together sharing our single mission.

I felt the clouds of the past cloak me, and I was barely treading water against the tide of my memories and of this date one year ago and the fear of what lay ahead of us. The weight of my entrenchment overpowered me. I realized I would have to build the emotional muscles to disengage, but not yet. Not until after the surgery.

I stayed for birthday cake and left as soon I could slip away.

AGAIN

*D*ear Nora,

    You are sleeping here in our living room. I put your little portable crib next to the front window so that when you wake you can see your favorite tree, which today is the color of apples—Granny Smith and Golden Delicious. It's raining. October rain makes it a great day for a snooze.

    You have a cold, but you are in your usual good spirits. I am worried. With the surgery only ten days from today, you must be completely healthy or they will postpone it. I am doing all I can to stay healthy, too. I can't let anything keep me from being with you in the hospital.

    I am very happy to think we could be nearing the end of your seizures. I am afraid to hope and also afraid to have you go through surgery again. When you are with me, it's easy to get lost in the joy of being with you. When you are not, I stay sane by avoiding thoughts of the future.

The future became the present too soon.

7:30 p.m. We were back in the hospital housing in Boston. Tomorrow would be surgery day. Tracey, Glenn, Wade and I carried the dead weight of our respective emotions, made heavier by the familiarity of this abnormal routine. We gathered in the house's community kitchen. The ugly fluorescent lights made my stomach even sicker than it already was. I held pajama-clad Nora on my lap, helpless against my need to hug her too frequently. I chattered and played with her, which helped me avoid thinking.

Glenn came for Nora, taking her to the lounge for her final feeding of the night, and Wade accompanied them. Tracey and I hung out in the kitchen, eating junk food that neither tasted nor felt good; it didn't fill the hole of our apprehension.

Throughout the evening, we'd taken a few pictures and I took one of the three of them in the lounge. A week prior, Tracey had photos taken of Nora. When I looked at those photos, I realized how plump Nora had gotten. Her weight, by design, was intended to fortify her for the surgery. She looked very healthy. It hurt to know that in a few hours all that would change. Knowing that beforehand made it even more difficult than the first time. We knew we'd just be glad to see her in recovery, regardless of how she looked. We endured the extra discomfort of knowing what to expect, yet not knowing what to expect, which compelled us to go through the motions of normalcy.

This time Wade and I had taken a more convenient hotel room across from the hospital, so at dawn we would only have to walk across the street. *Didn't we just do this yesterday?* I felt like I was dreaming, unable to discern these happenings from those of the January surgery. Everything was the same, except that Nora had grown, and perhaps that we had some knowledge of what we could endure. Expectations were both friend and foe.

As we waited, I held Nora for a while. I wondered if she tuned into my nervous energy. I searched her face for clues; she yielded none.

Nora had been in so many hospitals and doctors' offices that she remained unfazed by the surroundings. Perhaps the energy of our anxiety was also familiar enough to seem normal, or maybe she knew something we didn't.

When the time came again to separate, it felt that everything was happening more quickly than last time. There was no lingering or one last goodbye for us.

I could feel that it was much more difficult for Tracey. There is a photo Glenn took of Tracey and Nora in pre-op. Again, in this photo, Tracey sits on the hospital bed and Nora sits between her legs, this time resting her back against Tracey's chest. Tracey's arms encircle Nora's as they both lean forward. I can tell they are singing and playing. *It's the waiting game of let's ignore where we are and make the most of this moment, until I must surrender you again.*

Wade and I were off to set up camp again, like expert hikers in the wilderness. We unhesitatingly chose the same spot in the far corner, near the windows of the big waiting room. It was familiar and I chose it again because it seemed a "luckier" choice than trying something new.

The longer we remained alone, the more I wondered what was going on in pre-op. I was armed with food, reading materials and my laptop, but again I couldn't focus on them. This definitely didn't get any easier. I was already exhausted.

The day continued to loop, replaying events from nine months earlier; an odd kind of gestation period had transpired since then, but the birthing of this day was the same. We were braced for another painfully long "labor." Who would she be when she "arrived" this time? Who would we be?

Dear Nora,

Here we are again, at the end of the long room, camped out against the corner windows. After this, let's stay away from here, okay?

It's raining violently today. The walls of windows are spattered with wet. Drops slither and smear the glass like angry tears and the city trees below are fighting with the wind. Swishing branches and blowing leaves are one of my favorite scenes, but today it's all just a depiction of the fear and unrest we all feel.

I've dreaded this since the day we left here last time, but I made it back. We are closer than ever, except that now we feel the passage of every minute. We are moving forward only because you are leading us.

I love you, Nora, and can't wait until we can play again. No one, no child, no parent or grandparent should have to go through this. See you soon.

Now fully into the waiting game, I recognized that I also played head games with myself. I used history and expectations to pace my endurance, by telling myself that we would be there, as we were last time, until night closed in on us. My internal antagonist challenged me, secretly holding the hope that today would be simpler and shorter. I used this duality to keep my Libra nature balanced and, if nothing else, it meant that either way I couldn't lose.

Tracey and Glenn finally joined us at around 9 a.m. I could see that leaving Nora was clearly more difficult than before. Nora was no longer an unaware baby; she was a little, emotionally-connected person. Tracey told me Nora was under and asleep when they left, and knowing that, I was as relieved as I could be at that moment.

From her laptop, Tracey updated Nora's Carepage blog so others who waited for news would know what was happening. When she finally closed down, she did her best to shut out the day by stretching out on the chair-bed with pillow and blankets. Wade and Glenn peered with glazed intensity into laptop screens that I could not see from where I sat. I couldn't imagine what could hold their attention. From time to time I heard from them about spatters of communication with friends and family on e-mail. For me, it was a day punctuated by family text messages.

The ambassador-of-surgical-progress came and went every ninety minutes, with scripted news about the progress of the surgery. "All is well," she offered. I didn't believe her, though I hung onto every word of every report.

Around noon, Heather Plotkin from the Tyler Foundation appeared with her son, Tyler. Tyler is the foundation's namesake, and we were meeting him for the first time. He was a gentle five-year-old whose circumstances were somewhat different from Nora's, more involved and complicated. Heather and her husband Eric, who had visited us during Nora's first surgery, created the foundation that had helped with finances for Nora's medical and equipment bills. Again they offered hope, as well as gift certificates for meals, along with other goodies. With Heather was also her two-year-old daughter, Alyssa. I marveled that she found the time and energy to give so much to others.

After she left, we focused on food. Eating was more of a distraction than a matter of appetite and there was some temporary comfort in it.

We made it until 3 p.m., hoping that this time there would be no surprises. This hope was of no avail. The ambassador was approaching us, bypassing all the other families. As she spoke, I did not trust what I was hearing and my uncertainty was also reflected in Tracey's and Glenn's faces.

"The operation is complete," she said. "The surgeon is closing as we speak."

Happy tears sprung in disbelief. Could this be?

"Nora did really well; she didn't even need any additional blood," she added. "The doctor will be out to speak with you in about an hour."

Halleluiah! Of all the moments in fifteen months, this was the moment for which we'd waited. Letting go of any future concerns, this was moment that I dared to let down my guard. Nora was through and she was safe, and maybe she and we, wouldn't ever have to do this again. This was the first moment of its kind for Nora and for us.

This time, Nora's recovery was almost miraculous. We were able to see her in the ICU by 6 p.m. She was even awake, though very groggy and cranky. Crankiness was welcomed. It told us that she knew we were there and wanted to complain.

Mom's and Dad's voices and her favorite songs lulled her back to sleep. The nasty breathing tube was already gone and there were no drains springing out of the top of her head. The surgeon told us he was very pleased with the operation and how well Nora did. He had reattached the piece of bone in her head. She was moving as she always had and except for her bandage, she looked like our Nora, though there were still any number of other types of tubes and wires attached to her.

Everything we expected from the recovery process was compressed. Just three days later, on October 31st, we packed up the car and left for home. I sat in the back seat with Nora and she was as bright as she'd ever been and we were feeling that way, too. So far, no seizures at all.

TWITCHES

Back home after Nora's second surgery, I was not as exhausted as the first time, but I still felt drained. I was floating in happiness over Nora's rapid recovery, and was also ungrounded in my own ambitions. Relieved of the intensity of Nora's surgery, I wondered how I would get back to my own life.

I faced the chasm left by the absence of intense worry. The absence ironically provoked anxiety. I began to understand how some people unknowingly seek or cause new chaos in their lives, because chaos is familiar and provides focus. I also realized that this was not the first time I had experienced this feeling. In my life, prior to Wade's appearance in it, I had found purpose, even strength, in having to battle for most any small thing that I wanted. Resistance was presented in childhood by my father and repeated in my marriage. Wade, on the other hand, could not be a more supportive partner. He posed no resistance and when that disappeared, my ambition had gone with it. I discovered that adversity inspired me; without it, I felt lost. I needed to dig deep to unearth new purpose and ambition.

Now, the open and unclouded horizon was discomforting. With Nora's seizures eliminated, the focus could be on her development. Would she be able to walk? Would she learn to eat enough food to get her off tube feedings? Those questions only scratched the surface. I was still connected and committed to anything I could do to help, although it appeared I would be returning to a more predictable life and I knew that it would need to be different, because I was different. In the face of those feelings, I decided not to pressure myself, which was new behavior for me.

I gave myself the months of November and December to chill out. The economy and my work were both slow. I didn't care. If work landed in my lap, I did it; if it didn't, I showed up at my desk daily, but didn't put any effort into finding more.

The business of copywriting requires me to immerse myself in my clients' needs. I write for them by entrenching myself in their businesses and then projecting myself into the minds of the people they want to reach. The process requires a negation of self. My natural empathy had always been an asset, but now I was finding that part of me not easy to access. I no longer cared very much about what anyone else needed. Except for those closest to me, I really didn't give a damn. This was unlike me.

I began to feel an itch or an inner voice. I listened and let ideas come and go, shift and flow. The clarity of focus I had given to Nora, the concentration on the moment at hand that had sustained my sanity in the hospital with her, turned inward. The intense focus was now on me. What to do with me?

The Christmas holidays came and went. It felt good to flow with them, for maybe the first time since childhood.

NEW YEAR

December 31, 2009

Dear Nora,

It is New Year's Eve and what a year it has been!

This morning, we woke up together again. You might not think that's special, as we've woken up together many times in the past. But many of our awakenings have been in hospitals. There were some dark hours as we all traveled the bumpy, unmapped road in a territory your mom called "Noraville." In fact, one year ago today we were doing just that. It's wonderful that today we are in a better place, here at home.

You woke before it was light outside. I stole you out of the bedroom to bury us both in the comforter on the sofa. Held against me, you fell back to sleep. Even in the hospital we enjoyed times like that, when I could disconnect the wires that tethered you and cuddle you in the blankets of my lumpy bed which, by your presence, was transformed into a cloud of joy. Joy only comes momentarily. Cherish such moments.

I am painfully aware that the days of snuggling with you will be brief and I seize every opportunity for this. I drink you in and my eyes well up with such powerful emotions that I am at a loss to explain them, even to myself.

If you are reading this, you already know I wrote to you before you were born. I might have guessed we'd be where we are today, but I could never have anticipated where we'd have traveled in between.

January 16, 2010

Dear Nora,

One year ago today you were undergoing your first surgery. We were all in a state of suspended animation. For me, just taking a breath was painful. I can still access much of the fear I felt. I know that isn't living in this present moment, but sometimes I do it just to make sure I am fully aware and grateful for how good things are for us today. Enjoying this day for what it is is a choice I must make every day. The choice takes constant nurturing; it's a new level of consciousness and I have always been slow to awaken☺.

LOOKING

"When you change the way you look at things, the things you look at change." Wayne Dyer.

Having given no attention to my business throughout Nora's first eighteen months of life, the absence of client work found me staring into another black hole. I countered with the logistical challenges of cleaning out my files and reorganizing. In the process, I found some documents I'd saved from a workshop I'd attended some years before, given by a friend and life coach I'd known for years.

I realized that I hadn't seen Kim or heard from her in quite some time. Her handout was titled, "Eleven Reasons Why People Fail". I'd kept it because the reasons resonated with me. At the time I received it from her, saving the list was the only action I was able to take.

Still feeling much the same way, I tacked the list onto my bulletin board where I could see it, though I had no conscious intentions for it. It just felt like a good idea. A few days later, in what seemed like a coincidence, I came across some information that I thought Kim might be interested in. I called her, and we met for coffee.

Kim is a dynamic person and an attentive listener. I told her about Nora and how the experience brought me to my current state of searching. She invited me to participate in her three-day, intensive personal development workshop the very next weekend. I cleared my schedule, feeling this was an opportunity I couldn't miss. This turned out to be true—when the student is ready, the teacher appears.

Kim's workshop was titled, "Unlock the Genie". Her premise was that, "Success is your birthright", meaning that we all come into this world whole, complete and perfect, but we operate in the shadows of the meanings we attach to our experiences. Ultimately, we end up feeling we are much less than perfect. Like the genie of the lamp, we need to be set free. First, we must let go of the meanings we have attached to our back stories. Then, we are free to reconnect to our perfection and the power we've been taught to ignore. When we learn to work and flow within "Life's Laws", we can draw upon the magic of our most empowered true selves.

What I learned caused me to realize that, years before, I had lost more than my mother. I'd lost myself.

I had always believed that there is magic in life, even though I'd never experienced it in mine until Nora was born. Nora had definitely reawakened something in me. From that, I believe my inner guide had surfaced, drawing me to Kim and this workshop.

What I learned that weekend was how childhood experiences, like my mother's death and the meanings with which I had labeled it, had limited me. I discovered that these meanings become a person's beliefs, or paradigms, by which we shape our own lives. In reality, some of the beliefs I held were actually only choices I had made from conclusions I had drawn. I was awakened to the personal realization that what happens just is, but the meanings we assign to our experiences often run our lives forever. I came to see that my inability to let go of them was a big theme throughout my life.

I discovered I had lived my whole life according to a childhood misconception, formed soon after my mother's death, that, because she was gone and everyone was sad, that it was not alright for me to be happy. In my grief, I decided that if I were happy it was somehow being disloyal to my mother. Perpetuating the sadness served to keep her close. What it meant throughout my life was an inability to pursue my own happiness. Looking back from that vantage point, I sadly realized that I had projected and suffered this same feeling of disloyalty as recently as the year before, when I struggled to enjoy my son's wedding while Tracey was in the hospital. While I might have been expected to be upset, feeling disloyal as I did was acting in the shadow of an unconscious decision I had made long before.

Also rooted in my childhood loss was an inability to share my grief or talk about those feelings, because any mention of my mother would make my father cry, which was too awful for me to endure. It kept me stuck in unrealistic beliefs about happiness, while it also reinforced in me a feeling that I always needed to check to see how others felt before paying attention to my own feelings. To this day, it is still difficult for me to discuss or express how I feel. Writing is easier.

Probably worst of all, I'd decided asking for help was a sign of weakness. This came from a single incident. "We don't need any help," I'd heard my father say to someone on the phone, during those first few crucial weeks of grief. In truth, I did need help and the isolation turned me inward. I coped by labeling it as self-reliance. The simple truth was that my interpretation of these events became the foundation for some lifelong behaviors that held me back from becoming who I was meant to be. All of these reactions imprisoned or trammeled me in some way and wounded my self-esteem. I had been a child of great imagination and an adult who believed in magic, but couldn't access it. The magic couldn't find me because I was shackled by my feelings, all of which added up to unworthiness.

My "Unlock the Genie" adventure introduced me to the idea that it was possible to exchange limiting beliefs for ones that would empower me. This idea cracked open my shell. What poured out was profoundly tender. First, I had to accept that what happened was all that happened; the rest was something I had interpreted and misinterpreted. No blame was attached, but I had to let go of the regret that my life lessons came at such a great expense to me. I woke up to the idea that, regardless of what I once believed, if I could live with this new perspective, I could set out on a new journey and recreate my future.

A New Chapter

March 15, 2010

Dear Nora,

You inspire me. You've caused me to tap into a well of feeling I had lost. Were you sent to teach? Was that the message to me on the day you were born? All I know is that I was lost and somehow, through you, I am found. It is a connection of the most expansive nature.

All the times that I was with you and your mom throughout the ordeal of hospital visits, it was painful, and yet there was a deep joy in being with you. It wasn't sacrifice on my part; it was a strange gift. I do not wish to imply that I would have chosen for you to endure what you have so that I could grow in my own right. I would have given my life if I could have ensured you would not have had to do so. I do believe, Nora, that you are a gift to the world. Do not let anyone dissuade you from being who you are.

Today I started my book, Waking Up with Nora.

SCALE

Nora loves music. Ever since she'd noticed how Nora rocked her infant seat to the beat of the music, Tracey had begun to explore music programs for Nora. Just before her second surgery, she enrolled Nora in a Suzuki Music program. The Suzuki teaching method turned out to be more structured than made sense for her at the time. Subsequently, Tracey found more appropriate classes. These music classes were Nora's first real peer-based social encounters and the first time she was integrated into the world of typically functioning children.

The most visible difference was that, at eighteen months of age, Nora could stand if she was supported, but was not able to walk. When the other children marched to the music, Nora would be left behind, unable to participate in the prancing and dancing along with them. Also, not having use of her right hand meant she could not hold both of the two-handed instruments, which was a problem with cymbals and such. Tracey and I were unprepared in how to address these issues in the class. How did we facilitate the best experience for her? We fought our own feelings and our ignorance, too.

Until that point in our cloistered world, Nora was just Nora. What she could and couldn't do was just what it was. While her progress with her therapies was encouraging, dealing with the external world was outside of our scope. Now we had to confront it and the faces of other parents and children. They did not know us or have any idea how far we'd come from where we'd started. They couldn't know how happy we were that Nora was seizure-free. They had no way of knowing that where they saw a handicap, we saw a miracle. I imagined that all they could see were the differences between Nora and their children. Trying to view us through their eyes was the first time I'd faced this contrast.

It also was the first time I was aware of what it was like to make other people feel uncomfortable. I saw their questioning looks ... what was wrong with Nora? Why couldn't she walk? What had happened to her hand? Why did she seem slow? It initially buried me under a ton of new emotions. I was reminded of how cruel childhood can be for those who are different. I remembered, too, how I'd once overheard some educators discussing the aggravations and pitfalls of having special-needs children in their classrooms. Suddenly, it all became personal; a direct jab to the heart of me, and it stung.

Nora was oblivious to everything but her delight in the room full of children, the music and instruments; she was pure joy to watch. In contrast, Tracey and I were emotionally off-kilter and we earned our "sea legs" as a pair, taking Nora to the classes together.

I wanted Tracey to enjoy it as any mother should. I wanted to make things alright and protect them, too. The pain in my desire made me fierce. All Nora needed were my legs to carry her through the dancing portion of the class. I could do that. We could certainly help her hold the instruments or help her learn her own way of participating. In comparison to what we'd been through, this was nothing. Without a doubt, Nora was the most delighted, happy, eager child in the group. I needed no more incentive to join her or carry her, just energy and physical strength.

Still, there were times when my anger would flash. Rather than give into it, I fought against it with an intense focus on Nora's glee. Ashamedly, I admit, there were times I wanted to stop the class and say, *Hey, no matter what you may think, you only have average kids; we have a miracle.* I'd never utter such thoughts; I was ashamed that I had them, but the power of my anger helped me when I needed strength. I used it, and still do from time to time.

To be honest, everyone we encountered was really kind. The problem was mine, the judgment self-inflicted. But I was aware that it might not always be that way. The world is big and some minds are small. I realized the judgment about differences had the potential to become an issue for Nora as she grew in awareness. I knew I would have to find my place with it in this new world before I could really help her. I realized the best plan was to do all I could to help her become the incredible person she was meant to be. In those moments, I simply focused on her and celebrated

her uniqueness. That was easy; the rest would follow—I just knew it
would.

THERAPY

From the time Nora was two months old, she had been receiving physical therapy. In the beginning, this was three times a week. Tina was her physical therapist, the first of the three therapists to come into our homes to work with Nora. Along the way, Tracey engaged other therapies and therapists as well. The calendar was always jammed with appointments.

Around Nora's one-year mark, Elena, Nora's occupational therapist, began visiting to concentrate on improving Nora's ability to use her right arm and hand. It was just after Nora's second surgery that Sara, her speech therapist, came on board to address the oral issues that still stood in the way of Nora's eating.

Finally, by around the age of twenty months, Nora had progressed to being able to go from lying to sitting up on her own. She was crawling in her unique way, learning to coordinate her right side with her left. Her right leg was more functional than her right arm, so, though she was reasonably balanced on her knees, the challenge in crawling was getting her to bear weight on her right arm and open her hand against the floor. Most children do these things at six months. Being far behind in typical development, we all wondered if it was crazy to expect that she would ever walk on her own.

Along with her therapists, Nora had help from different types of equipment. As she grew, she had custom-made shoes and braces to provide support and balance, as she worked on learning to stand and to strengthen her legs. She had a removable arm constraint for her left arm to encourage her to use her right. She had a custom-made stroller, costing as much as a used car, to keep her torso aligned and her back supported on excursions. There was also her "stander," into which she was strapped and supported in a standing position for thirty to sixty minutes at a time. This served to strengthen her legs. In addition, there was her gait trainer, a bulky, specialized, highly adjustable walking aid with wheels. It was designed to support her while allowing her to propel the walker forward with each step. Nora was twenty months old and I remember the first time Tina strapped her into it.

We were all at Tracey's house and Tina was intently adjusting the gait trainer to fit Nora. Nora stood within the confines of the apparatus, curious but accepting the new experience and enjoying the rapt attention she was receiving. She waited patiently for Tina to tune and re-tune the many adjustments required to size it to her frame. Tina buckled Nora's little torso into the padded girdle-like support, being careful to avoid causing discomfort to her belly where the g-tube protruded. She wrapped the Velcro tethers around each of Nora's ankles. These tethers would restrain Nora's feet, keeping them beneath her and restricting them so that they could only move within a small radius...the radius of a single, child-sized step (hence the name, "gait trainer"). Finally all adjustments were made, and as soon as Tina released the brakes that secured the wheels, it took only a few seconds for Nora to put herself in motion with a minimum of prompting from us. I have no idea how she knew how, but Nora "got it". She took off down the hallway with great excitement. We cheered, applauded and shed tears of relief-driven joy, excitement and new hope for what might be possible.

At almost six months seizure-free, Nora remained on anti-seizure medications and would continue on them for another year or more; she would need to be gradually weaned off of them. It was really not possible to tell if or how they affected her strength or her coordination. And because she was still getting all her nourishment via tube feedings, we had no idea how her mouth, tongue or swallowing had been impacted by her brain surgery, or if she even had feeling on the right side of her mouth. There really are no tests for that and I doubted Tracey would have put her through them even if there were. Though she was rapidly learning to talk, Nora still wasn't interested in drinking or eating. Many people we know believed that all she needed was a taste of ice cream or some other treat and she would latch onto food. Not so. Nora's reaction to food was always the same; she was simply not interested.

With time, memory fades and I wanted to make sure that if Nora chose to, she should have the opportunity to know more about her accomplishments at this age, and the people who had helped her along the way.

Dear Nora,

Your therapists play such an important role in your life and in all our lives. Your mom and I are very fond of them, as you are. I hope they remain our friends for a long time, but one never knows, so I am writing this now because I think it is important for you to know something about each one of them.

Tina is your physical therapist. Of all your therapists, Tina has been working with you longest. I think Tina came into our lives when you were about two months old and she visits two or three times a week at your house, or mine if you are with me for the day. She was our introduction to learning the process of therapy. She had a demanding job! At first, it felt a little strange to invite her into our homes and allow her close physical access to you, but it soon became comforting, for it was apparent she is a very special person.

I am sure there are better clinical definitions of what physical therapists do and maybe by the time you read this you will know this firsthand. What Tina did was help you to connect with your body and help you develop a more purposeful, functional use of it. She helped you learn to roll over, sit up, crawl-- now she's teaching you how to stand and beginning to work with you on the process of walking. She stretches your body, your limits and your capabilities. What is wonderful is that she is as excited about every little bit of progress as we are. Tina was first to show us how simple toys could be masterful tools of therapy. She taught you songs that became powerful motivators. As with all your therapists, play is purposeful. You and Tina worked hard and played hard.

From Tina I learned that every baby has to learn what you are learning, and that simple games like "This Little Piggy" actually help babies strengthen the connections between their fingers and their brains. Your therapies do that, too, and they take into consideration your specific challenges, your life with seizures, post-surgical considerations, being medicated, your diminished muscle tone and alterations in how your brain maps to your body. Despite all that, what you are accomplishing is exciting and Tina has had a special hand in it.

Elena is your occupational therapist. OTs help people learn the skills they need to get along in daily life. Primarily, Elena focuses on helping you strengthen and use your right hand. It wasn't long after Elena came along that you learned that the words, "Use rightie," meant you were being prompted to use your right hand for a task as opposed to your left, which was easier for you. You were pretty amazing at one year old in being able to recognize your right hand from your left.

We have a removable left-arm-and-hand restraint for you, so that you must use your right arm and hand. When Elena comes, you graciously and sweetly place your arm in it and remain patient while she secures the Velcro straps that hold it on.

Elena also works to improve the dexterity of your left hand and encourages you to use both hands together. She always carries a big "bag of tricks" with her. This bag contains a wonderful assortment of everyday things that magically become tools of therapy. You covet the bag on every visit, wanting to dig into its treasures.

What's sweet about Elena is the lyrical tone of her voice when she reminds you, at least twenty-five times a visit to "use rightie". The enthusiasm she brings to every session and activity make it seem as if you are the first child that she's ever taught. She is a gift for us all.

Sarah is your speech therapist. From the time you were an infant, you always exhibited an extraordinary desire to communicate. Very early on, despite all the medications that likely clouded your world, your little eyes would zero in on our mouths as we spoke. The sheer desire to respond in like fashion to the sound of "Ah" would put your entire body in motion in an effort to summon the resources of your voice. So why speech therapy, you might wonder?

Speech therapy involves using the muscles of your mouth efficiently. For you, eating is the big concern. That's where Sarah comes in. Of all the therapists, she has to deal with the most confrontational therapy for you, because after your surgery you really don't like things in your mouth, so you are missing out on all of the oral stimulation and strengthening that naturally happens when babies eat.

This therapy was a big unknown to us. You had had a few sessions with another therapist before Sarah, and I had a really difficult time with her approach. When Sarah came along, everything changed. What a relief! It seems that in no time at all she's gotten you first to tolerate and then to accept what the rest of us have tried to do, but failed at.

Sarah was instrumental in getting you to eat from a spoon. Believe it or not, you had lost the ability to suck, but Sarah is teaching you to drink from a straw. Learning to chew will be next. You probably said "No" to Sarah more than to any of the other therapists. Sarah is petite, but she has vibrant energy. You seem to match each other in the kind of explosive excitement that you share for having fun.

STRENGTH

As Nora grew taller and heavier, caring for her for an entire day began to require more strength, because some of the simplest tasks became more physically challenging. The average child around the age of two can climb into and out of his or her car seat with a little help. Two-year-olds can stand beside your car and wait for you to grab a bag of groceries and then, in a flash, can beat you to the front door. They can travel a good distance on their own two feet; they can walk with you to the doctor's office or the grocery store. They move easily from room to room and up onto a sofa. Of course, this also means that they often fall down and bump heads and knees, but they are, thankfully, very pliable and relatively close to the ground, evidence of the fine developmental engineering in the human body's design and growth plan.

Nora was still unable to physically do many typical two-year-old activities. Lifting her twenty-five-pound frame as many as thirty times a day was very taxing. Strategy came into play when such lifting involved another maneuver, such as getting her into and out of the car seat, or in and out of the bathtub. Both required precarious back and arm extensions and good counterbalance from the adult. At bath time, because Nora was unable to stand unsupported, I'd have to lift her from a seated position on the floor directly into a seated position in the tub. I needed to be on my knees to accomplish this, which meant lifting her above my waist then leaning over the side of the tub to place her there. Lifting her out was the same in reverse. I'd dry her off on a towel on the floor. Afterwards I'd have to deploy a strategy to get the both of us off the floor without losing my balance. Overall, my concern was to be strong enough to do all this without injury to either of us.

Enter Nora's life-affirming influence on my physical fitness. I am usually self-motivated but, when it comes to exercise, I know I can't do one more sit up than is comfortable; I wimp out. I enjoy physical work; for instance, when we were renovating our home or landscaping, I had often surprised myself by handling, carrying and successfully moving weights much heavier than I would have expected. I hadn't done that for quite some time and my strength had diminished, and while Nora is a powerful motivator for me, it didn't extend to pushing myself to do workouts. The thought of a personal trainer crossed my mind; someone to be accountable to and to push me, except that I couldn't afford it. I was still curious. I stopped at a local gym just to check it out. The owner was there and he asked me what I did for a living, which rarely happens. It turned out that he needed a few newsworthy articles written and we bartered services. That's how I began strength training with a personal trainer

I have to say I hated the training. Of a different mindset than typical pumping-iron enthusiasts, at this gym they focused first on improving my balance and core strength. They understood the symmetrical inequities most of us have, and my workouts were designed accordingly. The strength and determination required to keep showing up and subjecting my body to pain and my ego to the humiliation of shaking muscles, sweating and grunting in front of others wasn't easy. My body hurt for many weeks, but I was happy I was doing it. My reward wasn't how I looked because of it, but rather the ease I felt in lifting Nora's weight off the floor without fearing that I would hurt both of us.

Over and above that benefit, personal training also gave me a great appreciation and empathy for Nora and her physical therapy. I am unquestionably empathetic, but this was different. I became keenly aware of the importance of coordination, balance and the role that our senses play in accomplishing them. I had thought that I already understood Nora's challenges, but these workouts made me realize how much we asked of her on a daily basis. I realized that I certainly didn't have her intrepid spirit.

The challenge of the exercises I was given caused me to become much more aware of the network of muscles it takes to accomplish movements that we take for granted. The trainer didn't know about Nora, yet I was being taught how doing exercises in different ways would not only build strength—they would also be making new pathways and brain connections that would serve to help me become more physically and mentally agile.

Also, I was consistently reminded of the incongruity between the strength and coordination of my right and left sides, as I lay on my back clutching dumbbells that jerkily wobbled above my face and chest. Unlike Nora, I had both sides of my brain to help me. What a miracle the human brain is, that it can compensate and adjust and make new connections on its own. Still, it was difficult for me. It took so much energy, concentration, commitment and focus. When it was too difficult and I wanted to quit, I thought of Nora. I imagined how hard some of the simplest tasks are for her and how hard she worked at them. Who was I to complain?

BREATHE

In June, Nora returned to Boston with her parents for outpatient EEG testing and visits with the doctors there. I was finding it difficult to stay behind for many reasons.

Any visit to Boston caused us all anxiety and Tracey thoughtfully sent me text updates and photos of Nora, who charmed the doctors and delighted the technicians as they glued the wired connections to her head for the monitoring.

All the test results and feedback were good: No seizures. She was doing very well.

LETTING GO

It was July and the birthday party of our brilliant four-year-old grandson, Patrick. The party was at the Jump Zone, one of those indoor kid-friendly places full of inflated bouncy houses. Tracey, Nora and I arrived together. I unleashed Nora from the confines of her car seat, grateful for a few minutes of contact as we moved through the parking lot. At the same time, I could feel my anxiety building.

We walked in and came face-to-face with the world outside our bubble. It's that world of able children that ceases to exist when we are home. There were twelve four-year-olds darting around the huge space, throwing themselves in, out and about the many huge inflatable amusements. Would Nora ever have the pure pleasure of attacking this maze of fun with abandon as the others were doing? I feared for her safety among the flying arms and legs of the other children.

Tracey seemed to have the situation well in hand. She always seemed so certain; she wanted Nora to experience everything at the level she could. She was right. I was scared. *How will I learn to let go of this fear?* I tried not to let my inner struggle show.

I passed Nora up to Tracey, who was already inside one of the bouncy cages. I knew the sensory experience would be good for Nora. Tracey bounced Nora, who was seated; I hid, terrified, behind my camera, snapping shots. I was relieved when they came out, but it was short-lived. We moved on to another one. It was physically challenging, hoisting Nora up into Tracey's arms.

I needed to remember that we were there for Patrick. I kept pulling myself back, out of my thoughts and into the experience. I worried about dividing time and attention between the two grandchildren. *I must remember why I am here today. How do I cope with this? Do other people go through this? How do other parents and grandparents of special-needs children act under these circumstances?* My conflict was clear; I could not deprive Patrick, yet I could not ever equalize the inequity of Nora's challenges either. *This will overwhelm me if I let it.* I struggled to do what I had not yet managed to do naturally. I disengaged and found Patrick.

From there, I thought I was doing quite well. I rejoined Tracey and Nora in another empty cage where we were the only three, so it felt safer. I jumped a little for Nora; she bounced up on my rebound and we laughed. *I want her to have a joyous life. I want her to be better than me; I want her not to be afraid.*

Tracey ran off to have some time with Patrick; leaving me with Nora. Outside of our cage, we stood right next to the air-bloated ramp of a larger cage filled with jumping children. The ramp was the perfect height to allow Nora to stand at eye level with me as I supported her as she bounced on the ramp. She turned away from me to watch the children inside.

When a child exited the cage, he or she passed within arm's reach of Nora. As they did, she would reach out to try to touch each child. *Does she sense that they are engaged in motion beyond her capability? If not, she will have to face that someday; how will it shape her life?* I deliberately stopped this train of thought. There was no value in it. No value in being anywhere except in that moment. I felt a fierce realization that being where I could have some control over her experience was the best place for me. Later, I would have to face letting go of the comfort my clinging gave me. I held back my fear and the tears that pushed against the rims of my eyes. There was still a lot to learn.

About four weeks later, a few days before Nora's second birthday, Tracey asked me to accompany her to check out a local home daycare center. I was not happy about this whole idea. Tracey realized this, and I admired the fact that she still included me. I knew, despite my apprehension, she would do what she needed to do. I did consider that some unstructured time with other children might be really good for Nora.

I liked the idea that this daycare was in someone's home and there would be only a few children. However, Nora was still sustained by tube feedings. She was getting better at snacking, but not yet good with liquids.

I worried about having someone else handle the tube feedings. It would be so easy for another child to tug on the line and pull the portal out of Nora's belly. Heck, I had done it myself. I had accidentally picked Nora up out of the highchair without disconnecting her feeding tube from the pump. Luckily, I discovered it just after, when I lifted her shirt to change her; I saw the hole in her stomach where the portal was supposed to be! Remorse for possibly having hurt her soon replaced the shock, but I also knew it had to be reinserted quickly because the hole would begin to close rapidly. My knees went weak, but I remained as calm as I could for Nora's sake and called Tracey. She and Glenn were on their way out of state for an overnight stay. I felt terrible having to interrupt their much-needed retreat. Tracey calmly talked me through the process of reinserting the portal. It still terrifies me when I think about it. If I could be so careless, how could I trust anyone else?

Letting go is one of my biggest challenges. The roots of the fear are so entangled in feelings about abandonment, that sometimes I can't tell the difference. It's not only about having been emotionally abandoned; it's also feeling that, by letting go, I am abandoning others. Letting go is a fear of losing control and not wanting things to change. It is fear of the unknown— or worse yet, the fear of what I have convinced myself will happen. I need to fully realize that, no matter what I think I know, I really can't predict what will happen. What I have learned from Nora I must learn to use on her behalf.

I saw in the daycare setting that she was happy and brave and ready to explore on her own, in her own way. But, for the millionth time, I was helpless against the tears that sprang all too easily from some deep place within me.

It was my own separation anxiety, of course, not Nora's I was feeling. How often she shone light into the darkest parts of me. It was becoming so clear to me that Nora's presence in my life was somehow connected to my mother. The experience I had had on the way to the hospital the day of her birth was clearly some introduction to it. It was not necessary for me to look further or try to explain it. She touched something in me that nothing else ever had and, in that, she catalyzed the process of me becoming wholly connected to myself.

I realized then that, if I could not breakout out of my prison of need, I would hurt her and Tracey, as well. I knew I had to learn to let go so we could both move forward. I was grateful, though, that this time, letting go meant growth and not goodbye, and that this time it would be a series of steps, and that I would have the luxury of time in which to take them.

BENCHMARKS

The time came to take a tour of construction progress on the new NICU in Nora's birth hospital. After Nora was born, the hospital began the process of planning a new Neonatal Intensive Care Unit. Tracey and I were invited to participate in a parents' focus group. Because of my involvement with Nora, I was the only grandparent in the group. It felt good to think our input might create a better experience for others who would come there, especially those as unsuspecting as we were. I thought that contributing in this way might help heal some of the negative emotions we'd endured. Being part of the group meant we received sneak previews of the space while it was under construction.

It was August, again. Two years had passed. On this particular afternoon, I attended the tour without Tracey.

I got a chill when I drove past the slashes of the white X on the blacktop of the parking lot where Nora's helicopter had stood, and I was reminded of how ordinary it probably looked to most anyone else.

In the lobby, I met our tour guide and, while I was exchanging pleasantries, I also felt the shroud of the past. Though I'd been back to this hospital several times since, today something was different. Maybe it was the time of day and the way the August sun washed the lobby. Perhaps, it was again experiencing the way the moisture on my brow felt as it was cooled by the air-conditioned lobby that had been so often one of my waiting-it-out campsites.

Beyond the gathering tour group, I saw the chairs in which I had spent countless hours waiting for an event or the future to be defined. I smelled the coffee and resisted the memory of how it had always sloshed in the constant acid sea of my stomach. I didn't come to visit this; I came to go forward. Perhaps that I have even noticed these feelings is some measure of how far I have come.

CHOOSING

Recently, I read that when asked to name their life's desire, most people put being wealthy at the top of the list. When pressed to define what money would really mean to them, the answer is peace of mind. Yet, the author affirmed that, if given a choice between feeling peace or passion, most people would choose passion. The difference, as it was explained, is that peace of mind is what we seek when we have had enough of the trials of life, but being naturally creative, experience-hungry beings, what we really desire and long for is a life filled with the exhilaration of passion.

Here again is my teacher, Nora, now just two years old.

It's evening and we've enjoyed a day full of many activities. I made play out of therapeutic activities as best as I could without sacrificing fun. I encouraged her use of "rightie" and helped her take steps, supporting her in marching to a one two-one-two cadence. We sang songs and played with new sounds, and tried with a mixture of determination and nonchalance to get Nora to eat and drink. These are lovely, exhausting days for me.

After dinner, the accumulated peanut butter or food-of-the-day in her hair is more than we've gotten into her belly. A bath is a must. I love her two-year-old naked body. I am overcome sometimes by the perfection of her; she's long and lean, but not too lean. She has that two-year-old's selfless, radiant beauty. While the g-tube extension that interrupts that smooth contour of her belly might be considered ugly, it somehow renders her even more of a miracle in my arms.

Nora loves her bath. As I lower her into the tub, I hold on tight to compensate for her excitement, her flying feet and her lack of fear. She sits, then slides down from sitting to lying down in one swift motion, a motion I have learned to anticipate and brace myself for, so I do not lose hold of her. She is fearless in the water. She loves lying flat on her back, letting it cover her ears. As soon as she's down, she prompts me to sing the "fishy song," our bath time serenade. I sing, and she smiles and fills in the missing words when I pause.

She is small enough that there's room in the tub when she's lying down to swish her body back and forth, swirling the water around her. She lies relaxed in my arms. Ever since mom and dad performed her first head-over-sink hair-washing at a week old in the NICU to wash the glue out of her hair after her first EEG, she has loved water and having her hair washed. What a kid! She plays and splashes about, but this child who still won't drink anything from a cup, insists instead on sucking on the soaking wet washcloth, swallowing some of the water. I don't stop her as I likely would have with any other child.

I know that bath time is over when she begins to take the toys and the soaked washcloth and fling them over the side of the tub, soaking me and the floor.

I lift her out of the water and plant her butt on the towel I've spread on the floor. She sits, her body and appendages now wrapped in a neat terry-cloth package. Holding a hand towel above her head, I ask, "Shall we do shoe shine?" She responds, "Yes," in giggles. Stretching the towel over the top of her head, with quick back and forth motions, I "shine" her head, drying her hair in the process. "Shoeshine, shoeshine, shoeshine," I repeat to her explosions of laughter. "More," she urges and I repeat this several times until I can no longer stand not scooping her up with my own giggles and hugs, while covering her neck with big smacky kisses.

Like any two-year-old, she is a bear to dress ... all arms and legs, completely committed to anything she can deliberately do to make diapering and dressing the ultimate challenge. By this time in the evening, I am wearing out. The routine is to let her watch her favorite TV show, which allows me to finish dressing her without a fight.

I plunk her towel-wrapped body on the blanket on the living room floor. The on click of the TV snaps her to attention. In the time it takes for the show to start, she looks back and forth several times between my face and the television, as if to question the sincerity of my promise. The show starts and she is riveted. Her body then relaxes. I finish dressing her and brushing her damp hair. Her gaze never leaves the screen.

I am delighted by the almost-spiritual satisfaction that her clean, pajama-clad body gives me. Still sitting on the floor, I move back a few feet to give her some well-earned physical and emotional space. She's transfixed until the story loosens its hold enough for her to want to change her position. Then she scoots back to lean against me.

Now I can look down directly over her face and, as I do, I can see down through the so-crystal-blue-as-to-be-transparent outer ring of her eyes. As I am captured for the millionth time by their beauty, she barely shifts her gaze.

I lift her up to sit on my thighs and she leans against my chest; I am captivated. I do not give into the urge to tighten my hug, too afraid it will break the spell.

These are some of my most cherished moments. They are rich with emotion that can only be known "by heart". I inhale them, memorizing what I will draw on for a lifetime. Twenty solid minutes of cuddling, each moment made more precious by the same one-moment-at-a-time realization Nora taught me during those difficult days and nights of her seizures and hospital stays.

My cell phone beeps and I know it's Tracey, texting me that she is on her way. I have only another fifteen minutes. I spend three of them as carefully as I would my last three dollars, certain I have well invested in the luxury I love most.

When I relinquish the moment, I call Wade to come away from his office to stay with Nora while I search the house, collecting and packing her feeding machine and other things that must leave with her.

Through the window, I see Tracey's car pulling into the driveway as I re-enter the living room where Wade is stretched out on the floor next to Nora. They are intently engaged in play. The sound of the front door opening snaps Nora to attention; she turns and when Tracey appears, they simultaneously light up like Christmas trees at the sight of each other.

"Hi, Peanut," says Tracey. "How's my girl?"

Nora goes into her excited, arm-flapping mode. Happiness.

A few minutes later, after my full report of the day's activities, the two of them are out the door. Wade and I walk with them to the car. We watch and wave as they drive away. Even though this all happens so often and should be routine, it never becomes any easier to see them go.

Back inside, I close the door and fold myself into Wade's arms, head on his chest. He knows what I am feeling; I know because I can feel that he feels it, too. How lucky we are. These good days are very good and I come to yet another realization. Sometimes peace of mind and passion are the same. Perhaps, I need not choose.

REFLECTION

"You will know that you have found your muse when you encounter a force that makes you feel courageous enough to broaden the range of your creativity."
From: *The Daily OM*

"When did you realize your passion?" asks the television host of his guest. The celebrity launches into her story and I lift off into my own thoughts.

It was mid-October in 1960, fifth grade, Mrs. Ruskin's class. The assignment was writing: *Write a story about Halloween.*

Looking back at my entire childhood, this is the only homework assignment I can remember. I wasn't a particularly good student; I cared more about being caught not knowing an answer or being reprimanded than I did about learning. Not being embarrassed in class was my only motivation for doing homework. But this assignment was different. It sparked in me then what I now recognize as desire … that tingling energy that won't allow your feelings to settle or be pushed aside.

That day, I could not find a story in me. I was then only one month into motherless-ness and the life lesson of how to live without my safety net. My vivid imagination had been rendered powerless. Imagination hurt too much because flights of fancy always dead-ended in the reality that my mother was gone.

My sixteen-year-old brother, the intellectual idol in my life, had already impressed in me a fascination for his ability to think, long before it became a coined phrase, outside the box. He was my best creative resource and I tapped him. Crossing the line between helping and doing it for me, he took my disjointed sentences and vague ideas and molded them into a story that I viewed as brilliant prose, complete with suspense and a surprise ending. I was hooked. I felt the exhilaration of riding the wave of words and their power to create pure magic. I knew it wasn't my creation. The teacher likely knew it, too, but probably overlooked it in light of my recent personal trauma. She gave me an A+. Even though it wasn't really mine, it became part of my story. Now, more than fifty years later, I still have that paper.

It was that moment that I knew I'd found something that was right for me. I didn't know what to call it, but I knew the feeling was special. From then on, writing was what I turned to when I hurt or felt joyful. It was secret and safe. It was a world away from the world I was in. I began to dream about writing braver and larger things that others would read. A book. But, dreams coming true had no place in my reality, they were only for other people, not me.

Over the years, I had dabbled in writing. I took a few workshops and classes. I did well, encouraged by my teachers to do more, but it still wasn't enough to make me pursue my innermost dream. Instead, I ended up melding my talent into copywriting for businesses. That seemed logical and natural. It wasn't about me; it was serving other people.

I think we've all heard that a true passion has a life of its own and cannot be ignored. That may be true, but I think it also has to be nurtured like a flower, or kicked out of the nest like a bird learning to fly in order to be realized. For me, getting from the dream to the realization of a passion took fifty years and a miracle named Nora.

Is it a coincidence that my fifth-grade homework assignment came a mere month after my mother's death? Was writing the answer to something bigger in my life? Was it my opportunity to be courageous? Was it a gift meant to save me? My tool for self-discovery in her absence? And why did it take me so long? Were there other signs I'd missed along the way? Probably.

Throughout my awakenings, catalyzed by Nora, I have come to adopt the belief that we choose to come into this life purposefully. We come for the experience, perhaps also seeking particular experiences. I know that Nora has played a huge role in what I came here to learn. I would never say she came here for me, though I do believe she is a natural teacher and is a connection to something much larger than what can be discerned through my narration of this experience. She challenged me so deeply that it caused me to dig for what I had lost and what I had not realized lay buried in me. She not only exhumed my desire to write and gave me this book, but she also caused me to discover and reassemble pieces of me I had lost. I could mourn the years that passed, or mourn the path that we all had to take, but there is no value in that. I choose to celebrate Nora and my discoveries. I believe that each of us comes to this realm to create the best life we can in every moment. With these letters on this page, I believe I am finally doing one of the things I came here to do. In spite of everything, I found my way. Would I have done it without Nora?

EPILOGUE

August 2014

It has taken me four years to bring this book to reality, and the experience continues to be life changing.

I have come to see quite clearly that we who love Nora see her as a miracle, where others may see her as handicapped. From that I have been inspired to carry that message of perspective to a bigger audience. While my goal is to use this book to raise money for "special" children, I also intend to pursue speaking engagements to raise awareness of the difference a simple change in perspective can make. My message is that if we can put down the lens of judgment, which only serves to keep us separate, we may begin to see that while we all are unique, we are all alike in our need to be accepted. Compassion is the key. Compassion requires no action, only a change of perspective, a change of heart that carries to the bloodstream of our lives a refreshing and life-enhancing energy. When you view others compassionately, you do a kindness to yourself as well. When you embrace a compassionate viewpoint, you immediately feel the release of the negativity and the stress it generates in your body. Compassion is a release and surrender of judgment, of others and eventually yourself. What you focus on expands, and when you offer acceptance, you will also receive it. This is not a new concept, but it needs to be repeated. It may be the one and only way each of us can contribute to creating a kinder world.

Nora Now

Just prior to publication, Nora celebrated her sixth birthday. She's walking, jumping and almost running, all have been goals of hers. She's just started kindergarten after an extra year of pre-school. When she first attended pre-school, she was only three years old, unable to walk without support and was still on tube feedings. Tracey exhibited such bravery in letting her go. I accompanied them to pre-school orientation, but when it came time for the first day of school and the first day that Nora rode the bus to school, Tracey and I agreed that I would not be included; because, try as I do, I am still far too emotional about separations. Thankfully, more than three years later, the bus driver says she's never seen a kid so excited to go to school every day.

Nora is pure light and she shines it on everyone, her teachers, therapists, doctors and literally everyone she meets. She talks up a storm, bosses all of us around, knows her alphabet, can count easily past 20, loves computer time and knows how to use the TV remote control better than I do. She amazes and humbles us with her enthusiasm and determination. She loves to laugh and gives us multiple reasons to do it with her every day. She still loves music and, like most of her contemporaries, loves taking selfies with our cell phone cameras and looking at the pictures and videos of herself.

When she hears that someone has been hospitalized, she asks if they, too, have had leads (EEG connections) put on their heads; she now is aware of the process having gone through it several times since her surgery as part of her checkups. She's also seen photos of herself in the hospital; though, she doesn't know her entire story yet, and that has given me more than a few sleepless nights. I am concerned about sharing her story before she fully knows it.

At around the age of three-and-a-half, Nora began asking me to tell her about when she was a baby. She asks me almost every time I am with her. I am always careful about what I tell her, leaving the tender details to her parents to present when the time is right. It's funny though, that Nora never asks her mother or anyone else; she only asks me. Is it because she somehow knows that the details of her past have remained very alive in me during my years of writing and re-writing this book? I can only guess. She continues to support my belief that she is in some way connected to something beyond our worldly scope, as when at mealtime, she nonchalantly leans over her chair, looks under the dinner table and matter-of-factly announces with joy, "Tilly's here," speaking of our beloved, deceased dog. And I can never forget that at the age of four she gave me chills when, with a far-off look in her eyes, she told me quite simply that "N-O-R-A spells God."

Nora still has many challenges to face; agility, compromised vision, learning to compensate for not having use of her right hand, just to name a few. She wears special shoes, a leg brace on her right leg, has many hours of therapy each week and more than the average number of doctor's appointments. Tracey and Glenn work hard to make sure she has what she needs. We know that as the loved ones of a "hemi" child we are always grateful and never home free.

In the eyes of the world, Nora may always be different, as many challenged and atypical children are. While the world may label them "Special", I know that, as do their parents and grandparents, these children aren't special; they are extraordinary and they humble and inspire us to find something of the same in ourselves.

2011, Tracey, Nora (3 years old), Tanya
Photo by: Hanlon

Resources

Hemispherectomy Foundation
www.hemifoundation.org
Dedicated to children and families who are impacted by
hemispherectomy brain surgery

Tyler Foundation
www.tylerfoundation.org
Dedicated to helping improve the quality of life for families affected
by epilepsy

The Brain Recovery Project
www.brainrecoveryproject.org
Funding research that is key to understanding the tremendous
neuroplasticity of the brain

Children's Hemiplegia and Stroke Association
www.chasa.org
The Children's Hemiplegia and Stroke Association (CHASA) exists
to help children – children who have survived an early brain injury
that results in hemiplegia or hemiparesis (weakness on one side of the
body). We also help adults who have been living with a diagnosis of
hemiplegia since childhood.

The Epilepsy Foundation
www.epilepsy.org
Epilepsy and seizures helpline: 1-800-332-1000
The mission of the Epilepsy Foundation is to stop seizures and
SUDEP, find a cure and overcome the challenges created by epilepsy
through efforts including education, advocacy and research to
accelerate ideas into therapies.

About the Author

Tanya Detrik is an award-winning writer, marketing communications copywriter, author and speaker.

She is the mother of two, and is the delighted grandmother of four girls and one boy. She lives in Connecticut with Wade Caszatt, her partner of more than 20 years. Her articles have been published in regional and national home design magazines. *Waking Up With Nora* is her first book.

She can be reached at author@wakingupwithnora.com.

42603031R00123

Made in the USA
Middletown, DE
16 April 2017